A House of Meanings

A House of Meanings

Christian Worship in Plain Language

Juan Oliver

CHURCH
PUBLISHING
INCORPORATED

Unless otherwise noted, the Old Testament quotations contained herein are
from the New Revised Standard Version Bible, copyright © 1989 by the Di-
vision of Christian Education of the National Council of Churches of Christ
in the U.S.A. Used by permission. All rights reserved.

Unless otherwise noted, New Testament quotations contained herein are from
David Bentley Hart, The New Testament (New Haven: Yale University Press,
2017). Used by permission.

Church Publishing
19 East 34th Street
New York, NY 10016
www.churchpublishing.org

Cover design by Jennifer Kopec, 2Pug Design
Typeset by Denise Hoff

Library of Congress Cataloging-in-Publication Data
Names: Oliver, Juan M. C., author.
Title: A house of meanings : Christian worship in plain language / Juan
    Oliver.
Identifiers: LCCN 2019038880 (print) | LCCN 2019038881 (ebook) |
    ISBN 9781640651401 (paperback) | ISBN 9781640651418 (ebook)
Subjects: LCSH: Public worship.
Classification: LCC BV15 .O46 2020 (print) | LCC BV15 (ebook) |
    DDC 264--dc23
LC record available at https://lccn.loc.gov/2019038880
LC ebook record available at https://lccn.loc.gov/2019038881

Contents

Wisdom has built herself a house;
she has carved her seven pillars.
She has prepared her food, spiced her wine,
and she has set her table.
She has sent out her young girls [with invitations];
she calls from the heights of the city,
"Whoever is unsure of himself, turn in here!"
To someone weak-willed she says,
"Come and eat my food!
Drink the wine I have mixed!
Don't stay unsure of yourself, but live!
Walk in the way of understanding!"

Proverbs 9:1–6

Preface

One of the most fulfilling experiences of my pastoral ministry has been the exploration, with the recently baptized or their parents and sponsors, of the meaning of their experience of that sacrament and the eucharist. To these sessions we invite anyone who wishes to come and listen to the conversation. In the process, I am always stunned by how those who have just joined the household of God repeat, entirely unawares, ancient wisdom about the meaning of our rites. This ancient wisdom resides in a house—the Bible, of course, but also the worship of the Church. I have written this book to invite you into that conversation, to explore this house together.

Theology, if it is indeed "faith seeking understanding," assumes an experience of faith. In the case of *liturgical* theology, it is an experience of faith in and through worship.[1] Thus, any faithful worshipper can engage in a more or less disciplined reflection upon the meaning(s) of their experience in liturgy. Yet I have often been baffled by the absence of that reflection in many parishes. We very rarely explore together the meanings of our worship experience—too often we leave it to the priest and her sermons to do the trick. But a sermon is not an extended conversation.

Welcome to *A House of Meanings*. Although you may read it by yourself, this book is structured in a way that begs for open sharing in a series of parish forums, ideally during the seven weeks of Easter. Each chapter corresponds to a week, beginning with Palm Sunday and concluding on the week after Pentecost. Each begins with the readers' experiences of worship, and then brings into the conversation aspects of our centuries-old accumulated wisdom regarding worship. In this way, I am inviting your own experience to come into dialogue with the rich deposit of insights from tradition. In practice, this means that you—or the group—should read the first chapter during Holy Week, the second during the first week of Easter, the third during the second week of Easter, and so forth, the early chapters reflecting on the liturgies that you have just experienced, ending on the week following Pentecost Sunday.

---

1   Anselm of Canterbury, Proslogion 1.

Making selections from the vast library of the meanings of Christian worship is a daunting task. I have concentrated on early church writings until about 650 CE for a main reason: The early Church, although full of local variations in practice, was a single Church, undivided until it split in the eleventh century into East and West, along a line going from Egypt through the Adriatic and up through the Slavic countries.

The unified cultural world of the Mediterranean quickly fragmented. By 650 CE communication between East and West had become sketchy. Rome, which had a million and a half inhabitants in the second century, dwindled to a population of twelve thousand by the end of the fifth and remained very small, with only a slow increase during the Renaissance, until it soared after the Industrial Revolution. Cows grazed in the Roman Forum throughout the Middle Ages.

Western Christian intellectual life shifted to the monasteries and did not begin to pick up until Charlemagne's efforts to improve education in the ninth century and later, during the High Middle Ages, *after* the separation of East and West in 1057. For these reasons, then, most of my references will be to the undivided Church in the first seven centuries. In the process, it is my hope that our ancient understandings of worship might be more widely shared, freed as much as possible from the professional academic terminology often inaccessible to the average person.

I am grateful to the great cloud of witnesses who reflected upon their experience of worship during the first seven centuries and wrote down their thoughts. Also to every teacher, mentor, and conversation partner who has helped me to reflect and explore my own experience in the light of theirs—especially liturgy professors at the Graduate Theological Union in Berkeley, California, the members of the Council of the Associated Parishes for Liturgy and Mission, and the leadership of the North American Association for the Catechumenate, as well as colleagues in the International Anglican Liturgical Consultation and the North American Academy of Liturgy. My deepest thanks go to Professors Louis Weil, Andrew McGowan, Nathan Jennings, James Turrell, and James Farwell, who read parts of the manuscript and offered valuable suggestions. Any errors still remaining are my own.

Special thanks also go to my editor Nancy Bryan, and the team at Church Publishing, Inc., who patiently and firmly encouraged the project from the beginning and consistently improved the work with suggestions. Finally, thanks above all to my spouse, Johnny Lorenzo, without whose patience and enduring support this book would have never seen the light of day.

The people of St. Bede's Episcopal Church in Santa Fe, New Mexico, endured my ranting, musing, and probing as we began to develop these chapters in community during Easter, 2018. Well done, good and faithful people! This book is dedicated to you.

Chapter I

Signs of Grace

How Worship Works

The sacraments are outward and visible signs of inward and spiritual grace, given by Christ as sure and certain means by which we receive that grace.[1]

For some time now you have been exploring life as a Christian. I say exploring because the process is never-ending—life in Christ is that rich. Throughout, you may have struggled with difficult issues like the meaning of Bible passages, the brokenness of the Church, and perhaps even your own brokenness and God's never ending love and compassion for us and all creation.

You have also engaged in an ever-deepening relationship with God, both in intimate solitude and in worship shared with others. You have joined other Christians and other groups in our work of love and compassion for the neediest, combating the structural causes of poverty, suffering, disease, and environmental degradation in our time. These also are aspects of being a mature Christian.

---

1 The Book of Common Prayer (hereafter BCP), 857.

Throughout all this, though, you may have won-
dered about the meanings of worship.

Like any human action repeated over thousands
of years, the Christian worship of God has come to
contain words, phrases, and ideas that increasingly
seem unclear, preposterous, even fatuous. It is not
surprising that they have become obscure and perhaps even unintelligible to some of us and certainly to non-Christians. Additionally, our society is, by
leaps and bounds, quickly forgetting the spiritual
dimension of life. Some try to fill this very real absence by exotic forms of worship, from another time
and another place. Others reject it out of hand, ending up understanding worship as little more than a
social get-together. Instead, I invite you to join me in
exploring the deep meanings of Christian worship—
meanings profoundly human *and divine* developed
through our worship practices in the first centuries
of our existence as the Church.

Most of my life I have been enthralled, excited,
moved, mystified, and annoyed by Christian worship. Still, I find it, like God, an inexhaustible source
of meanings. I say meanings in the plural because,
as I hope you will discover, the meaning of worship
is never a single thing, but a multiplicity of meanings, layered together into a rich, complex experience that can transform us and sustain us as we
grow spiritually, individually, and as communities
of faith.

Often we think that the meaning of something is somehow given, official, or universal, singular. But as Lutheran liturgical scholar Michael Aune wrote, meanings are always meanings-to-someone.[2] That someone, in this book, is not me, but *you*. You will be discovering and elaborating the meaning of worship for *you*; in the process, I will be bringing out, from storage, as it were, the meanings of worship to *us*, the Christian community over the earliest centuries for you to engage in dialogue with the sources of our tradition.

Personal and shared meaning. This book is about the meanings of worship. In the romance languages derived from Latin, meaning is translated as "significance"—what something signifies, as Aune notes, "to someone." So it is one thing to look up the meaning of baptism in order to find out what the Episcopal Church thinks it means officially, and a whole other thing to share the meaning of your child's baptism with your friends over a cup of coffee. One meaning is official and formal, even doctrinal. Yours is yours. *We should not assume that therefore yours is less real.* It may or may not agree with the meaning to the rest of us as larger community have framed, in which case conversation may be encouraged and sought out.

---

2 Michael B. Aune, "Worship in an Age of Subjectivism Revisited," *Worship* 65 (1991): 225. For the expression "meanings-to-some-one," see Ronald Grimes, *Ritual Criticism* (Columbia, SC: The University of South Carolina Press,1990), 42.

In this light we can expect Christian liturgy to have as many meanings as there are worshippers! And yet, the doctrinal meanings of liturgy rose through time precisely out of personal meanings shared, discussed, and argued about until we could come to a more or less *shared* meaning.

Liturgical meaning, therefore, is much more common and widespread than what a theology student reads in a library. Of course, a person might still go to church to socialize or hear beautiful music, or out of just plain boredom and depression. In those cases, the meaning of the event to them is different from the meaning of eucharistic worship to the wider Church.

Ritualization. Worship is a form of human ritualization. We humans ritualize all over the place, for all sorts of reasons. From the scheduled football game to the family gathering at Grandma's for Sunday dinner, to graduations, birthdays, and so forth. We set apart a time and place to do something meaningful to us in a more or less structured way. These events, tiny or very grand, are *patterned*: they have norms, musts and must nots, even a history. They identify us as part of a larger whole, whether it be a team, network, family, neighborhood, or community. So Christian ritualization or worship is action at a place and time set apart, involving musts and must nots, with a history and layers of meanings.

Worship, made up of signifying actions, creates a meaningful experience. It does *not* do this, for the most part, by presenting us with ideas, but by engaging participants in *patterned behavior*—and so ritual is much more about doing than about saying. Throughout this book, therefore, we will be trying to link the actions (including texts) that we carry out in worship to what it means both to us individually and as a community travelling through time, landscapes, and cultures.

It used to be thought that ritual communicates ideas and myths (that is, stories with a meaning). After all, it is full of them. This was the general view toward the end of the nineteenth century. Later, however, Clifford Geertz discovered that rituals not only convey ideas, but form in us an *ethos* and *worldview*.[3] Ethos is a specific "flavor" or way of behaving. Worldview is a community's understanding (intellectual *and affective*) of the world as it is and their place in it. So rituals present to the participants a felt sense (not only understood) of what their life in the world should look and feel like: the proper way to live. It is because of this ritualization of "the proper way" that participants can know when they fall short of it. Additionally, ritual action often integrates our constant failure to live the ideal life through purifications, forgiveness, renewals, and closures.

---

3 These terms are defined in Clifford Geertz. "Ethos and World View and the Analysis of Sacred Symbols," *The Interpretation of Cultures* (New York: Basic Books), 126 ff.

The sacred. Religious rituals especially have a way of presenting themselves as *sacred and authoritative,* sanctioning different aspects of the community's life. These rituals crown kings and ordain religious leaders, join couples in marriage, and deal properly with human remains.

The sacredness of religious ritual is facilitated, if not downright constructed, by taking place at a place and time cut off—even if temporarily—from every-day "profane" life and declared to be sacred precise-ly because it is set apart. Thus student of ritual Jon-athan Z. Smith pointed out that a thing, person, or event becomes sacred through "emplacement"—by *taking place* in a *sacred context.*[4] The chalice at the eucharist, for example, is not sacred because of its design or costly metal but because it is employed in a sacred action.

We can, of course, find other experiences in life "sacred" beyond ritual, directly, as it were. Rudolf Otto referred to these experiences as "numinous" —an experience of divinity—which *may* appear in worship, but may also just as well appear in nature, in relationships, and throughout all our lives. It is the human experience of *transcendence,* of there be-ing more to life than what is apparent.[5]

---

4   Jonathan Z Smith, *To Take Place: Toward Theory in Ritual* (Chicago: The University of Chicago Press, 1987).

5   Rudolf Otto, *The Idea of the Holy* (Oxford, UK: Oxford University Press, 2011).

At the core of religious ritual, then, is the sacred as a place and time set apart from the "profane." But the sacred place is actually the same as the profane, only demarcated as sacred *by ritual action,* whether it is the consecration of a church or the circle formed by worshipers celebrating the eucharist at a picnic table in the woods. This is important, for one goal of ritual is to reveal that all of reality is sacred, sending us back to it to experience everything as holy, and live accordingly.

Signs. Our lives are full of them. Not only traffic signs, but also much richer, complex sign-actions, like sharing a meal or a hug. Signs are always *expressions of something beyond themselves.* They always have two parts: the sign (arms around a person, for example) and what is signified (friendship or love). In our exploration we will try to keep both poles in balance: the *sign* and what is *signified.*

Some signs mean univocally; that is, they are designed to convey a single meaning. A red octagon with STOP on it directly conveys an order to stop your vehicle, without any other possible interpretation. Others convey meaning more indirectly, with multiple resonances and meanings. A birthday party, for example means much more than "you are older now"; it also means "we appreciate and love you, we are happy you exist," and so forth.

Our worship is a system of sign-actions, or to put it more grammatically, *signifying acts,* which *must*

carry meaning for the participants in order to signify. If—for example—in order to hug you, I must
explain what a hug is, hugging is not working well as
a sign. Signs work best when they easily and without
explanation lead us to the signified. So the sign actions in worship need to be clear, and graspable, by
both our minds and hearts.

In order for signs to work as signs, we must engage them analogically. An analogy is a comparison
based on a similarity. If I said, "The forest is covering the hill as my green shirt is covering me," I
would be stating an analogy. Based on that comparison, however, I might say, poetically, "The hill wears
a green shirt." The latter is a metaphor, based on my
earlier analogy. Of course, the hill is doing nothing
of the sort, since the forest is not clothing, but the
reader gets the point of comparison *immediately*,
through a compressed analogy, that is, a metaphor.
In this example "shirt" has become a sign for "forest." It would be sheer silliness, however, to take
the metaphor *literally* and demand to know whether the forest is made of cotton fabric! As moderns,
our increasing inability to think poetically drives
us to think only literally, making our experience of
sign-actions increasingly difficult. The water of baptism, for example, can remain just water, bearing no
further freight of meaning. We cannot see it as the
waters of the Flood, the Red Sea, and the River Jordan as its blessing prayer suggests. For those with a

literal bend eating and drinking bread and wine in memory of Jesus is just that: the bread is just bread, the wine just wine. They do not *signify* and make present Christ, whose Body we are as a community. If understood literally, the bread and wine only make themselves present, and thus *do not work as signs,* but point only to themselves. In today's world, where many consider only empirical data real, leaving out subjectivity (meaning, feeling, memory, and so forth), it is increasingly difficult for many to see something as a sign or icon that makes present what it signifies. For the ancients, however, the sign or icon made the signified *present.* Instead, too often now what to them was a world shining with mutual references, is opaque to us.

The stuff of signs. Our signifying actions in worship are human actions, and so they are *embodied,* for worship does not consist only of sharing ideas, but of doing something in a specific place, decorating it perhaps, moving, engaging objects, gesturing, washing, eating, anointing, keeping silence, singing, and speaking—all things related to or done by our *bodies.*

We can't very well gather to only *think* about God, without anything visible. If we could, the Church would be a sort of collection of preserved brains, a thing for science fiction. Like it or not, we need visible, tangible, physical sign-actions in order to have liturgy, even if it consists only of bodies sitting together to meditate. Perhaps this is why the Orthodox sing, celebrating the triumph of Orthodoxy over those who would destroy icons,

> No one could circumscribe the Word of the Father; but when He took flesh from you, O Mother of God, He accepted to be circumscribed, and restored our fallen image to its former beauty. We confess and proclaim our salvation in words and images.[6]

It is precisely thanks to the enfleshment of God in Jesus that we can and must use physical signs to live our spiritual lives physically, audibly, visually, incarnationally. This is why worship cannot be only a sharing of ideas, but an event in which bodies do signifying actions. In worship the "spiritual" is also physical, so much so that Pope Leo the Great would write that ". . . what had been visible in Christ [his body], after the ascension, became the sacraments of the Church."[7]

Engaging the sign in faith. What does it take to be able to "read" the sign-actions and enter into them? St. Thomas Aquinas, commenting on the classical

---

6 Orthodox Kontakion for the first Sunday of Lent, Sunday of the Triumph of Orthodoxy.

7 Leo the Great, Sermon on the Ascension, 74.

definition of sacraments at the head of this chapter, pointed out that as outward signs sacraments effect inward grace given our proper *disposition in faith.* We are so accustomed to the word *faith* meaning the assent of our minds to an unprovable claim that we have lost the full meaning of the Greek term *pistis,* which means, rather, trusting allegiance—a much fuller resonance, closer to "the trust of my heart," or "confidently relying on." This meaning may be best captured by our use of the word followed by "in," as in, "I have faith *in* you, son." Faith in this sense is the trust of the whole person (mind and feelings) in the object of trust, in this case, God. You may have noticed, for example, that in the Creed we do not say, "We believe *that. . .*" but, "we believe *in. . . .*"

The sacraments, then, convey God's grace to the participants as they *put the trust of their heart in God.* Our ability to engage a sacramental sign always involves trust in God and God's gracious action through worship and what it signifies. If we have no faith in God, nor care at all who Jesus Christ was, if we think the eucharist is simply another social gathering, and do not have any trust in its ability to re-present or manifest Christ among us, the sacrament is still the sacrament, but we cannot open up to the grace that it brings about in us. For God's self-offering to us is there all the time, but God will not force us to accept the free gift of grace. We must open its door with a trusting faith.

At the very least, faithful allegiance involves our suspending disbelief, like spectators at a play. We trust in what the signs represent, holding in tension *both* the knowledge that we are participating in sign-actions, *and* at the same time experiencing the realities that they signify.

Worship, then is made up of sign-actions, which are at the same time both a sign and the reality they make present. This was beautifully explained to me by six-year-old Stephanie, in the wisest sacramental insight I have ever heard. When I asked her, "Tell me, what is the bread we eat here?" She proudly recited, "The bread on the altar is the Body of Christ." Then she hesitated, thinking, and added, "Well, it isn't, but it is."

Grace. Our catechism definition says that sacraments are signs of inner *grace*. Christian conceptions of grace, however, bear little resemblance to the way we use the term to mean beauty, charm, or attractiveness. In Greek, grace (*charis*) means gift, and therefore in theology, grace is God's free *(unearned)* gift toward us. That is, God's love for God's creation—all of it, not only humans. In this way the sacraments are a main way in which our participation in the life of God is revealed, named, acknowledged, and made stronger. Grace is not a thing, or a commodity to be dispensed, but *God's own loving self-giving to us*. We can now fill out the definition of sacraments a bit further:

Sacraments are visible, physical, external Christian sign-actions through which God's own divine life is shared with the participants given their disposition in trusting faith.

A sign of what? What does the Christian community's significant actions in worship represent as a whole? Let me suggest for now that our gathering to worship God makes present, not only God, but our vision of life lived with and in God's presence—what the gospels call "the kingdom, or reign, of God": that is, *this world* as God would have it, restored and healed in truth, justice, peace, and love.

Christian worship is a sign of God's reign, even though that reign has obviously not arrived among us yet. The coming Reign of God is made present and actual to us *via* the system of signs that is worship—and we can be aware of both at the same time, much as six-year-old Stephanie wisely noticed.

Further, our ritual enactment of the reign is *formative,* for in worship we learn the attitudes (worldview) and behaviors (ethos) proper to the Reign of God and are formed in them by enacting it as it would look and feel if it were to arrive here and now.

Sacrament and liturgy. Finally, since we use the terms "sacrament" and 'liturgy" quite often, let me explain their origins and meaning. In the third century Tertullian wrote that a Christian soldier could not take an oath of loyalty to the emperor, a *sacramentum,* because in baptism he had already taken one to Jesus Christ. This is how we got "sacrament" in Western Christianity. In the Eastern Churches, however, the term has always been *mysterion,* or mystery. But it does not mean something unknown, like the murderer in a who-done-it. Rather a *mysterion* (from *mus,* or shhhh!) in this context is a rite about which one keeps quiet, for it can only be experienced properly by those prepared to engage it through a process of instruction and transformation. When St. Jerome translated the Bible into Latin he translated *mysterion* as *sacramentum.*

Whether sacraments or mysteries, the sign-actions of the Christian community take place in the context of *liturgy.* Originally, the term did not mean anything like ritual. In the ancient Greek city-states citizens had the obligation to do work (*orge*) for the welfare of *all* the people (*laos*). They might pave a road, build a bridge or equip a company of soldiers for a war. This activity was termed *leitourgia.* So liturgy was, first and foremost, work done on *behalf of the people* and their well-being. "Public works," if you will.

When the Hebrew Bible was translated into Greek, the Hebrew word *avodah* (service to God in the temple) was translated as *leitourgia.* And so liturgy came to mean both a service to the people and service to God. For these reasons "liturgy" refers not only to a Christian *worship service*, but also Christian work in service to the people—especially the poor, the sick, our planet, and so forth. For we are not to stay in church forever, but are always sent out to cooperate with God in the birthing of a new world—the Reign of God—and aware and thankful, we recognize God at work in every aspect of life, from the weed in the garden to the love of spouses.

This then, is the scope of *The House of Meanings*: we will be reflecting together on your—and the Church's—experience of worship. As ritual, our worship has many things in common with all the other rituals of humanity: it does what it does—create in us a shared ethos and worldview—by employing sign-actions that engage us in a rehearsal of God's coming reign of truth, justice, peace, and love. Since these actions are signs, they are meant to convey meaning and meaningfulness. For us to receive God's grace conveyed by these sacramental signs, we need to approach them with an open, trusting allegiance (faith) exercising a willing suspension of disbelief, to enter the sign and get to engage the depth of the sign's meanings. These sign-actions enable us to see and feel God's loving will to heal all of creation, and to know how God's reign will look and feel when it arrives. Equipped with this vision, and familiar with the signs of the Reign of God, we can go out into the world recognizing God already at work in it, joining in God's mission to heal it.

Finally, our system of sign-actions that is worship—all of it—stems from a historical event: the life, message, service, witness, arrest, torture, execution and ongoing life of a first-century Galilean itinerant rabbi, Jesus, the Anointed One (Messiah, or Christ). And so it is to the celebration of those events in Holy Week, that we now turn.

Chapter II

The Hinge of the Year

The Liturgies of Holy Week

Holy Week is the most important liturgical week of the year. During it we relive and explore the meanings of the foundational events that gave birth to the Christian community, the Church. Beginning with the Sunday of the Passion: Palm Sunday, and moving through Holy Monday, Tuesday, and Wednesday, to Maundy Thursday, Good Friday, Holy Saturday, and finally to Easter Day, we celebrate Christ's *Passover:* Jesus's passing through death to new life. Rather than explore your experiences of the main liturgies of Holy Week in one fell swoop, I suggest we do it one by one.

We begin, paradoxically, with Easter. Holy Week did not appear fully formed as an observance the day after Jesus rose from the dead. It took three hundred and fifty years for it to develop more or less into what we have today. Before there was a Good Friday observance, or a Maundy Thursday and Palm Sunday, the earliest Christians celebrated Easter. *Every single Sunday*, in the celebration of a shared meal, the eucharist, recognizing the risen Christ among us in the breaking of the bread.

Soon though, probably by the second century, a *yearly* celebration of Easter began to develop, held either on the date of the Jewish Passover or on a Sunday near it. It was a single celebration of *both* Jesus's death *and* his resurrection and consisted of an all-night vigil to recall and celebrate the whole event. By the late third century, however, death and resurrection had been split into two days—the Sunday of the Passion: Palm Sunday, and Easter Sunday.

The Sunday of the Passion: Palm Sunday

Your experience. Since this book is structured to begin with your experience, you may want to reflect on the following questions, either alone or in your group: What elements of Palm Sunday—what memories—come to mind, both good and problematic? Do you look forward to Palm Sunday? Why? What do you expect, how does it sometimes disappoint, what would you be missing if you did not participate? What does it mean to you? You may want to jot these down.

Passion Sunday. The word *passion* does not here refer to deep feeling, but comes from the Latin *passio,* suffering. Thus, the "Passion of Our Lord Jesus Christ" is the account of his suffering and death. This Sunday before Easter, which in Jerusalem included a procession with branches, had a totally different emphasis (possibly older) in the West: There the passion narrative was the *only* gospel reading on this day for seven hundred years.[1]

By the eighth century, though, Irish monks, probably influenced by Eastern liturgies, begin to process with branches in Northern Europe; but the gospel reading was still the Passion. Two centuries later the Western Church had added the procession with branches as a prelude to the eucharist—keeping the reading of the Passion, and it is so to this day in most of Western Christianity, expressing Eastern and Western roots in this day's official name, the Sunday of the Passion: Palm Sunday.

The procession with palms. In the East it was not until the emperors Constantine and Licinius made Christianity an acceptable religion free from persecution in 313 CE that our Holy Week observance began to grow, and its growth depended largely upon a very astute bishop, Cyril of Jerusalem, who quickly became the consummate religious tour guide.

Pilgrims began to arrive in Jerusalem and they kept coming and coming. One of them, a nun from a distant place—probably Gaul (central France)—kept a diary of her travels in the Holy Land and that is why we know how Cyril elaborated his tours-with-

---

1 For example, Augustine, in North Africa, preached on the Passion on this
   day, and so did Leo the Great in Rome in the mid fifth century.

worship. The trinket sellers, I like to think, adored him, as did the innkeepers and tavern managers.

In any case, our nun, Egeria, described Holy Week observances in Jerusalem around the year 380 CE in her diary, which survives. It is from her that we have our earliest description of Palm Sunday in Jerusalem:

> On the Lord's Day [Sunday] which be-
> gins the Easter Week, the people went
> to the main Church [the *Martyrium*] in
> the morning for Eucharist. At one in
> the afternoon all went to the Mount of
> Olives, and hymns, anthems, and les-
> sons were recited. At 5 PM they heard
> the story of how the children carrying
> olive branches and palms met Jesus,
> saying "Blessed is he that comes in the
> name of the Lord." And all went back
> into the city, shouting, "Blessed is He
> that comes in the name of the Lord."
> And all the children in the neighbour-
> hood, even those who are too young
> to walk, are carried by their parents
> on their shoulders, all of them bearing
> branches, some of palms and some of
> olives, and thus the bishop is escorted
> in the same manner as the Lord was of
> old. And they went to the Holy Sepul-

cher [*Anastasis*] to say evening prayer, and returned home.[2]

Notice that in Jerusalem the eucharist took place in the morning and the procession with palm and olive branches in the afternoon, leading to evening prayer.

The meanings of the Sunday of the Passion: Palm Sunday. In order to better understand the meanings of this Sunday it is helpful to first explore the meanings of executions and palms in first-century Judaea.

Jesus was by no means the only person in Jerusalem greeted by cheering crowds waving palms. So was, in all likelihood, the Roman governor, Pontius Pilate. It was a common sight in the Roman empire for arriving dignitaries to put on a grand entry into a city, whether as part of an inspection visit (*parousia*), to collect taxes, or to celebrate a triumph over enemies. Waving branches was fairly standard at these triumphal entrances. So it is not too far-fetched to imagine Pilate would have come into Jerusalem from his headquarters in Caesarea Philippi in a grand manner. Jesus was in all likelihood *mocking* this display of power as he enacted it, not by entering standing on a chariot all-powerful and grand, but on a donkey, cheered by children.

---

2 *Itinerarium Egeriae*, 30.

This means that our waving branches on this Sunday does not only proclaim Jesus as king, but also implies *that the powerful have no real power over us.* This mock triumph alone would have been reason enough to get Jesus arrested. But there is more.

Immediately after this "triumphal" entry on a donkey, the synoptic gospels report that Jesus went straight to the temple and drove out the money-changers, the sellers of animals, and their beasts. Their presence there was necessary and legitimate, for Roman coin could not be used in the temple precinct, though of course, the money-changers got a cut of every transaction. The sellers of animals were there legitimately too, in order to provide animals for sacrifices. Additionally, by eating with undesirables and proclaiming the free forgiveness of sins (without the need of repentance or sacrifice) Jesus incurred the wrath of the temple leadership. If a mock triumph were not enough, an assault on the temple and free forgiveness were. An arrest would be imminent.

So Palm Sunday is not simply about cheering Jesus our king, but about the *cost* of being obedient to God, to God's call for a life of truth-telling, justice-doing, peace-making, and love, which in the case of Jesus, involved courting trouble. At the beginning of the most important week, we are warned about the *cost of following Jesus as a citizen of God's coming reign of justice and peace,* as we hear in the second reading on this day:

Be of that mind in yourselves that was also in the Anointed One, Jesus, Who, being in God's form, did not deem being on equal terms with God a thing to be grasped, but instead emptied himself, taking a slave's form, coming to be in a likeness of human beings, and being found as a human being in shape, he reduced himself becoming obedient all the way to death, and death by a cross.

Philippians 2:5–8

Jesus did not die by accident. He was, in the eyes of Pilate, a dangerous zealot. He—or his followers—claimed him to be the descendant of King David, with a real claim on the throne. Except; he had a sense of humor, and so sat on a donkey instead of riding in a conqueror's chariot. I can see him smirking, raising his arm pompously to salute his followers, mocking the important people in Palestine. Then he went to the temple, created a ruckus, and paid dearly for it.

It is important, I think, to begin Holy Week by making a connection between Jesus's lifestyle, message and ministry, and his arrest and execution.[3] Let's not beat around the bush. Jesus did *dangerous* things, treating immigrants like citizens, eating

---

3 See James Farwell, "Salvation, the Life of Jesus, and the Eucharistic Prayer: An Anglican Reflection and Proposal," *Liturgy*, 31.3 (April 2016), 19–27.

with sinners and declaring the forgiveness of sins for free, without any need for repentance or temple sacrifices. If we had been priests there, we'd be worried about our livelihood, and of course, any insult to Rome was also an insult to the temple priesthood, in cahoots with the invaders. *He had to be stopped.*

It's even more dangerous, however, for Christians to worship an imperial Jesus, projecting our own grandiosity on him—full of power and majesty and followed by cheering crowds—without a single ounce of irony. Such a view of the "triumphal" entry is wishful thinking, hoping that we can share in his "triumph" without his cross; wanting to eat the cake of discipleship and have it too.

By "his cross," I mean suffering for the sake of *justice*. The shame and pain of the cross were the price Jesus paid for breaking rules, siding with the least and the destitute, getting in the face of the powerful, and above all, letting the religious hypocrites ("charlatans" in Greek) of his day have the full measure of his contempt for them. To his suffering, and in the light of it, we bring all our suffering, from toothaches to the loss of a child, and find meaning and healing for it.

So yes, we cheer at the beginning of Palm Sunday, but we do so trembling even as we sing hosannas. We get the memo: the cost of Jesus's obedience to God is also the possible cost of *our* obedience.

The *Triduum* or
Christian High Holy Days

Triduum (three days, pronounced TREE-doo-oom) is the Latin word usually employed to refer to Maundy Thursday, Good Friday, and Easter Vigil as a whole, for they make up a single celebration over three days. "Christian High Holy Days" will do as well. These are the most important liturgies of the whole year, and of them, the Great Vigil of Easter is queen. If you can attend only one service, go to the last one, the Vigil.

Recall how, starting in Jerusalem in the late fourth century, what we know as Holy Week began to develop as ritual reenactment of the stories in the gospels in their original settings. The tendency continued with the development of these three days.

Maundy Thursday, Holy Thursday,
or Thursday of the Lord's Supper

Your experience. Again, let us begin with your sense of the meaning of this day. What do you love about it? What memories does it bring up, both good and problematic? What would you be missing if you did not participate? What does it mean *to you*?

The beginning of the troubles. Since the Jewish—and liturgical—day begins at sunset, the Maundy Thursday liturgy, usually celebrated after sunset, is already on Good Friday. In bishop Cyril's Jerusalem, there was a non-stop liturgy overnight, processing to the places of Jesus's last supper, betrayal, arrest, torture, and "trial." The liturgy took a continuous form, but I like to think we eventually split these aspects up to get some sleep. Thus, our Maundy Thursday liturgy is the beginning of our celebration of Good Friday. In a sense, it is its eve.

The first three Gospels describe Jesus taking bread and wine on this night, as Jews do to this day when saying grace, saying the blessing, and declaring these to be his body handed over and his blood poured out as God's new covenant, turning the traditional Jewish grace at meals into a rite about his healing and liberating death.

The Gospel according to John, however, substitutes a story about Jesus washing feet. "Maundy" is a contraction of the Latin *mandatum,* or commandment, referring to Jesus's commandment, "Love one another as I have loved you," expressed by washing each other's feet and indicating that our lives are to be lives of loving service. So we wash each other's feet.

Although we are remembering the institution of the eucharist on this night, we do so in the context of the arrest, trial, torture, and execution of Jesus. We are not so much celebrating the Real Presence of Christ in the eucharist (a special celebration in Roman Catholicism on the feast of *Corpus Christi*)

as we are contemplating the connection between
our weekly eucharist *here, now, every Sunday,* and
his Passover *then* and *there on Good Friday.* Other
practices, like the watch before the reserved sacrament, and the stripping and washing of the altar,
are secondary, and therefore optional in the Book of
Common Prayer.

Optional reservation of the eucharistic bread and wine.
Consecrated bread and wine from the Maundy
Thursday eucharist may be reserved overnight if it
is to be shared at the next day's liturgy. Until the sev-
enth century, we had no eucharist on Good Friday
at all. This makes sense, since Good Friday is a day
of fasting and the eucharist is *always* a festive meal.
Some congregations today are returning to this earlier practice of abstaining from communion on Good
Friday. Others continue to share communion from
the reserved eucharistic bread and wine. These parishes may also observe the custom of reserving the
eucharistic bread and wine from Maundy Thursday,
and keeping a silent watch at the place of reservation. It is not appropriate to reserve the sacrament
for a vigil if it is not to be consumed the next day.

Optional stripping and washing of the altar. This optional custom, which developed as late as the ninth century in the West, involved the stripping and washing
of the altars and floors in the morning *prior* to the
Maundy Thursday liturgy that evening. It probably
originated in the practical need for cleaning up the

church before the *Triduum* began, but the action quickly became identified with the stripping of Jesus's garments on Golgotha. This understanding of liturgical actions as referring to specific moments in Jesus's life became fashionable at the time. As much as it is great theater, the stripping and washing of the altar also places the congregation already within the trauma of Calvary.

The shared supper. Some congregations, perhaps in an attempt to reclaim the supper nature of the eucharist, share a simple meal either before or after the Maundy Thursday liturgy. It should be noted that it is *not appropriate* to pretend that this meal is a Jewish Seder or to employ the prayers and recitations of the Seder, which is a Jewish liturgy belonging to the Jewish people. If a congregation wishes to experience a Seder, perhaps a local synagogue could invite the congregants to theirs. Alternatively, if we wish to stress the meal character of the eucharist, we may celebrate the Maundy Thursday eucharist at tables, entirely in the context of a full meal as Christians did for our first 160 years, while still observing the rubrics of the Holy Eucharist, or the Order for Eucharist.

Since the Maundy Thursday liturgy is only the first installment of a three-day liturgy, it ends without a dismissal, usually in silence.

The meanings of Maundy Thursday. Maundy Thursday invites us to enter into the meaning of every eucharist and its relation both to Jesus's life of loving service and its inevitable consequence, his suffering, death, and rising to new life to install his reign of justice and peace. Whatever form Jesus's last supper took, it occurred not only in the context of Passover, but in the more intimate context of a week fraught with peril and fear for Jesus and his close followers. Paul, writing to the congregation in Corinth only a generation after Jesus's death, told them,

> For from the Lord I received what I also delivered to you: that the Lord Jesus, on the night in which he was betrayed, took a loaf of bread, and having given thanks, broke it and said, "This is my body which is [being broken] for your sake. Do this for my remembrance. Likewise, after supper, the cup also, saying, "This cup is the new Covenant in my blood; do this, as often as you drink, for my remembrance." For as often as you eat the loaf and drink the cup you announce the Lord's death until he come.
>
> 1 Corinthians 11:23–26

This was the earliest understanding of the eucharist—it precedes the writing of the gospels—and links Jesus's Jewish grace prayed at his last meal to his death.

Writing to the Corinthian Christians (likely a house-church of less than thirty-five or forty people), Paul explains that by eating and drinking the "Lord's Supper," God is revealing that *they* are the Body of the risen Christ, and therefore must not abuse each other, as the rich were doing to the poor by eating separately from them. Already tonight we have glimmers of Easter.

Good Friday

Your experience. What does this day mean for you? What memories come up? What do you love most about it? What do you dislike? What is puzzling, weird, upsetting, or in need of exploring? What does the service(s) mean to you?

We have no records of a Good Friday liturgy until Egeria's accounts of practices in Jerusalem in the late fourth century. Soon after the building project decreed by Constantine, the legend developed that his mother, Helena, had found Jesus's actual, true cross. This was an extremely important motivation for pilgrims and architects alike, and so the Church of the Holy Apostles (*Martyrium*) led to the tip of Calvary hill behind it, surrounded by a large area leading in turn to the Resurrection Mausoleum (*Anastasis*) built over the site of Jesus's tomb.

Egeria describes Good Friday as taking place in stages. I have compressed her text and translated it into contemporary English:

Morning Prayer. Beginning before sunrise, people have come down with the bishop from the Mount of Olives, where they spent the night, and now at the *Martyrium*, have just heard the account of Christ before Pilate. The bishop encourages all and consoles them for their hard work and tells them to come back at ten for the veneration of the cross. But now, still before sunrise, they go to the Church of Sion [the "upper room"] to pray at the column where Jesus was scourged, and return to their houses for a while, but soon all are ready.

The Veneration of the Cross. [At ten] a chair is placed for the bishop in the *Martyrium*, he sits at a linen covered table and a silver-gilt casket is brought in, which is the wood of the Cross. The casket is opened and both the wood and the title [spelling out Jesus's charge] are placed upon the table. He holds the extremities of the wood firmly, while the deacons guard it, and the faithful and candidates for baptism pass through to kiss the wood. And because someone is said to have bitten off and stolen a piece, it is so guarded lest anyone approach-

ing should venture to do so again. . . .
All the people are passing through until
noon.

The Three Hours. At noon they gather at
the tip of Calvary hill, just behind the
Martyrium, a court of great size and of
some beauty; here all the people assemble in such great numbers that there is
no passing through. Lessons and hymns
show that what the prophets foretold
of the Lord's Passion had been fulfilled.
Prayers also suitable to the day are in-
terspersed throughout. The emotion
shown and the mourning by all the
people at every lesson and prayer is
wonderful; here is none, great or small,
who during those three hours, does not
lament more than can be conceived,
that the Lord had suffered those things
for us. Afterward, at three in the afternoon, there is read that passage from
the Gospel according to John where He
gave up the ghost. This read, prayer and
the dismissal follow.

Evening Office. [about three in the after-
noon]. When the dismissal has been
made, Evening Prayer is sung at the
martyrium, as is customary this week at

this hour, until late. And then they go to the *Anastasis,* where the gospel is read where Joseph of Arimathea begged the body of the Lord from Pilate and laid it in a new tomb. A prayer is said, the baptismal candidates are blessed, and the dismissal is made. Some stalwarts spend a second night in vigil at the Anastasis.

That was in Jerusalem, about 380 CE. In Rome, however, Good Friday did not originally include the veneration of the cross, concentrating instead on readings of and about the Passion, which had originally been part of the earlier one-night Easter observance before it was split.

The Book of Common Prayer (1979) recovered this liturgy. Mercifully, it also compressed it so it can be celebrated in about an hour. It is the official and principal liturgy of Good Friday. Other devotions such as the custom of listening to sermons for three hours and the Way of the Cross are optional, and may not take the place of this worship service.

Good Friday today. It is natural to think that when we celebrate Good Friday we are grieving and lamenting over Jesus's death, but that is not the whole story. The service is very simple. There are no decorations in the church at all, no candles, no linen cloths, and so forth. It begins starkly, with the ministers entering in silence and kneeling or prostrating in prayer.

Then the bishop or priest prays only asking God to "behold this your family..."—without asking for anything else. Readings are then heard (Isaiah 52:13–53:12 or Genesis 22:1–18 or Wisdom 2:1, 12–24) followed by Psalm 22:1–11(12–21) or 40:1–14 or 69:1–23. A second reading, from Hebrews 10:1–25, follows, and directly we hear the Passion according to John (18:1–19:37 or 19:1–37), which may be read with parts taken by different persons or chanted the same way. A sermon always follows, and then an optional hymn.

The ancient Solemn Prayers of the People remind us first that God sent his Son "not to condemn the world, but . . . to deliver us from the power of sin and death, and be heirs with him of his everlasting reign." We pray for the Church (all denominations), our unity, and those about to be baptized, by name; for all peoples and those in authority, for all who suffer in mind, body, or spirit, all who have not heard the Good News of God, and those who have persecuted others in Christ's name; for the dead and for ourselves, that we may be heirs to Christ's reign.

Optional veneration of the cross. A wooden cross may be venerated by the ministers and people. The manner in which this may take place may vary greatly from congregation to congregation. Three anthems are provided by the BCP to be sung or said during or after the veneration. None of them are mandatory, and any other suitable hymn(s) may replace them.

Optional communion In places where Holy Communion is to be administered, confession and absolution follow, then the Lord's Prayer, and the administration of communion.

The service ends with a prayer. There is no dismissal or blessing, for the liturgy continues on Saturday night with the Great Vigil of Easter.

The meanings of Good Friday. It is tempting to think of Good Friday as Jesus's funeral, given its sobriety, but it is not. It is part of the holistic three day celebration of Christ's *victory*. If on Thursday we center on the eucharist as the *re-membering* of that victory through a ritual meal, on Friday we concentrate on the cross as the *place* of victory, and the Easter Vigil luxuriates in our awareness of that victory and what it means for us and all of creation. Good Friday may be solemn, bare, and stark, but it is not a funeral; it includes celebration and yes, *joy*. Wearing red vestments is entirely appropriate.

To followers of the Way (the earliest name given to Christians) the crucifixion of Jesus came to have extraordinary significance, and they immediately began to develop an understanding of what God had been up to in Jesus's life, death, and in their experience of his new, continuing life among them.

Ransom. We noted earlier that the death of Jesus must not be disconnected from his life, which proclaimed in deeds and words the Good News of God's coming reign, living as if that reign had already arrived in which ". . . The blind see again, the lame walk, the deaf hear, lepers are being cleansed, and the deaf hear, the dead are raised and the poor are given good tidings" (Luke 7:22). The irony of it, though, was not lost on the first Christians. The king of this new Reign of God reigned from a cross, spat upon and bloodied, in agonizing pain.

Did it *have* to be this way? We moderns want to know. Are we glorifying violence?

No. God does not want violence. That is precisely why the Word came to rescue and heal a world suffering under violence. Our celebration of Good Friday is not a glorification of violence, let alone making suffering a badge of pride. Jesus could have simply taught, healed, and loved, dying of old age. But his deeds and words *set him against, and were a threat to,* those who inflicted violence, exploitation, and oppression. Siding with the oppressed, Jesus submitted to the very violence that victimized *them.* More recently, other pacifist leaders such as Gandhi, Martin Luther King, and Oscar Romero have followed suit, willing to suffer the victimization of the oppressed. This oppression of Jesus's contemporaries required relief, or *liberation.* From what? From abuse by the Romans and the temple priesthood, of course. But also from the "principalities and powers," which ancient peoples believed controlled the destiny of humans and whole nations.

These powers held the world in bondage to evil, destruction, and death. Like all slaves, our freedom from bondage had to be bought at a price, a "ransom." This ransom fee paid by Christ was *not paid to God*. Later theories of "atonement" distort this insight by suggesting that an accountant God required payment from Christ for the sins of the world. This is not what the New Testament claims. Rather, we celebrate the payment *by God*, to our enslavers, freeing us to join God in love and freedom.

Most of us do not see ourselves as slaves to evil and death. But the existence of oppression, evil, destruction, and death at the hands of powerful elites is ever on the evening news, and extremely real to the poorest among us. Even if we do not see the world and its controlling "powers that be" in this way, these realities are still very much with us today. Thus on Good Friday we celebrate liberation through a life and death in solidarity with those whose lives are a perennial wound.

In sum, Jesus died for the sins of the world not to pay *God* for your sins, but rather God, having become human out of love, paid, in his own body, the *price of our liberation from slavery to sin*, to free us from slavery to our own brokenness and the powers of evil and death, and *not* because God is a mean accountant demanding bloody payment from his own Son.

Holy Saturday

Your experience. Holy Saturday has its own liturgy, rarely experienced by most people, but you may want to reflect on the meaning of the day for you. What memories come up in relation to this day between Good Friday and Easter Day? Do you have any particular customs or observances? What do you dislike about it? What do you like? What is its meaning *to you?*

Meaning There is a beautiful fifth-century sermon by Epiphanius of Cyprus that captures the meanings of this day, between death and resurrection:

> What is happening? Today there is a great silence over the earth, a great silence, and stillness, a great silence because the King sleeps; the earth was in terror and was quiet, because God slept in the flesh and raised up those who were sleeping from the ages. God has died in the flesh, and the underworld has trembled.
>
> He goes to seek out our first parent like a lost sheep; he wishes to visit those who sit in darkness and in the shadow of death. He goes to free the prisoner Adam and his fellow-prisoner Eve from their pains, he who is God, and Adam's son.

The Lord goes in to them holding his victorious weapon, his cross. [He greets Adam] and grasping his hand he raises him up, saying: "Awake, O sleeper, and arise from the dead, and Christ shall give you light.

"I am your God, who for your sake became your son, who for you and your descendants now speak and command with authority those in prison: Come forth, and those in darkness: Have light, and those who sleep: Rise.

"I command you: Awake, sleeper, I have not made you to be held a prisoner in the underworld. Arise from the dead; I am the life of the dead. Arise, O man, work of my hands, arise, you who were fashioned in my image. Rise, let us go hence; for you in me and I in you, *together we are one undivided person.*

. . . "But arise, let us go hence. The enemy brought you out of the land of paradise; I will reinstate you, no longer in paradise, but on the throne of heaven. I denied you the tree of life, which was a figure, but now I myself am united to you, I who am life. I posted the cherubim to guard you as they would slaves;

> now I make the cherubim worship you
> as they would God.
>
> "The cherubim throne has been pre-
> pared, the bearers are ready and wait-
> ing, the bridal chamber is in order, the
> food is provided, the everlasting houses
> and rooms are in readiness; the trea-
> sures of good things have been opened;
> the kingdom of heaven has been pre-
> pared before the ages."[4]

Notice several things: It is not enough for Christ to save his contemporaries and those who came after him, he also rescues and heals all humanity going back to Adam and Eve. He not only rises to heaven, but goes down to the underworld to free even them from bondage to Satan ("the Accuser"). I do not know of a better theology of the connection between Good Friday and Easter, and the implications of the banquet that we celebrate every Sunday, the eucharist.

This reminds us of the corporate nature of Christ's saving death and new life. In our individualistic culture, we see events as happening to "me" more easily than to "us." But Christ's liberation of us is not only individual; it is also—perhaps even primarily—communal. We, all of humanity and all creation, are liberated from bondage to evil, death, and destruction. *If we want to be.*

---

4 Epiphanius of Cyprus, c. 405 CE. Emphases mine.

The Great Vigil of Easter

Your experience. That ancient, long, and rich service is next. What do you look forward to in the Easter Vigil on Holy Saturday night? What images does "Easter" bring up for you? What memories? What would you be missing if you did not participate? What meanings does it hold *for you?*

The last installment of our *Triduum* or three High Holy Days is the most ancient, dating definitely to the late second century. It has developed since to involve four parts: fire and light, ancient stories, baptism, and eucharist.

Fire and light. Since the Easter Vigil was originally an all-night affair, it begins with the service of light that began Evening Prayer. (Alternatively the same service may be celebrated as a sunrise service, but it must begin before sunrise, in the dark.) We gather in darkness around a new fire, and light the Easter candle, a symbol of Christ, light of the world, risen among us. The deacon sings an ancient Thanksgiving for the Light, or *Exsultet*, from its first word in Latin. It is a proclamation of Easter, declaring Christ to be the true Passover Lamb who passed over from death to life in order to liberate and heal his faithful people. Just as Moses led the Hebrews through the Red Sea, tonight Christ leads us through death to new life through the waters of baptism.

The ancient stories. Vigils are supposed to take time. So we listen and respond to at least two readings, one of which is always the Exodus account of God freeing the Hebrews from bondage through the Red Sea. Other readings from the Old Testament, such as the creation story, the sacrifice of Isaac, the valley of dry bones, Jonah in the whale, and so forth, may be read as well. All have something to say to us about the passage through death to new life, our spiritual journey of transformation in, with, and by Christ's own dying and rising.

Baptisms. Even if no baptisms are scheduled, we renew the promises we (or our parents and godparents) made at our baptism. The reading from Romans on this night spells out how, through baptism, we share in Christ's death and resurrection:

> Are you unaware that we—as many as were baptized into the Anointed One (Christ) Jesus, were baptized into his death? Thus, by baptism into death we were buried with him in order that, just as the Anointed was risen from the dead by the Father's glory, so we too might walk in newness of life. For if we have become planted with him by/in the image of his death, we shall at least also be [in the likeness] of his resurrection."
>
> Romans 6:3–5

We will explore baptism more fully in the next chapter.

Eucharist. We then make eucharist, proclaiming Christ's resurrection as his Risen Body through our own baptismal death and resurrection. We will explore the eucharist fully in chapter four.

Observances. There are many ways of celebrating the Easter Vigil. One can begin in the dark, after sunset. Or one can expand the service into an all-night affair, beginning with the liturgy of fire and light after sunset, and continuing with readings, meditations, prayers (and coffee breaks!) throughout the night; if so, congregants should feel free to come and go, or to join perhaps the beginning and end if they cannot stay up all night. In this case, the eucharist should begin about dawn. Alternatively, the service may begin before dawn, in the dark, and go into the morning.

In perhaps no other service of the year are our sacred doings as rich in meaning. We light a new fire, then a large candle, bringing it into the dark worship space to gradually share its light. We sing its praises as a sign of the risen Christ; we hear ancient stories and respond to them, maybe even sharing their meaning after each if the group is small. We wash new members in water that has been compared to the flood, the Red Sea, the river Jordan. We anoint those baptized with fragrant oil, and dress them in new clothes. We make eucharist, *the* Easter celebration *par excellence,* in which God manifests that we are the Body of the Risen Christ.

The Meanings of Holy Week

Our worship during this greatest week of the year can seduce us into travelling back in time and worshipping *there and then* rather than *here and now.* We can too easily imagine ourselves in first century Jerusalem, *watching* Jesus do his saving acts. And indeed, Bishop Cyril's attitude is still very much alive today. We want to "go back to the place" of the events of this week. Worship, however, is not time travel, but a series of doings here and now, through which we are shaped to live as the Body of Christ in the world *today.*

Christianity, if it lives in expectation of the coming Reign of God here, cannot be a religion of there and then, but of here and now. If worship transports us to an exotic "elsewhere" different from our contemporary lives, but does not shoot us right back to our current reality, it is mere liturgical tourism or even self-absorbed reverie. Instead we are invited to contemplate what happened then and there and listen to how it applies to the here and now. Which are the principalities and powers that keep us and all creation enslaved to evil and death *now*? How do we go about, with God's grace, to confront them

and demand to "let our people go"? Are we aware
of questions like "who is suffering in our neighborhood, *why*? Who is oppressed and exploited and *by
whom*? What shall our response be to all this evil?"
For we, too, and the whole world, can be raised with
Adam and Eve into the light of the Reign of God already beaming right now, among us. We, too, can die
to the old self and be raised again as individuals and
as communities.

Holy Week is a prolonged entering into the very
core of the mystery that is "Christ among us, the
hope of glory" (Colossians 1:27). From this core pour
out—as water and blood from the side of Christ—
baptism and eucharist and our whole life as Christians. It is who we are. It is how we become who we
are; it is how we grow into what we hope to be.

Chapter III

Your Own Death and Resurrection

Baptism and Confirmation

We have begun by exploring the liturgies of Holy Week, how they celebrate the core events and meanings of our lives as Christians, and ended by pointing toward baptism and eucharist. It is to these that we turn now and in the next chapter.

We begin with your experience. What has your experience of baptisms been like? What was wonderful? Telling? Puzzling? How did *you* become a Christian? If you cannot remember your baptism, think of the process by which you made an adult decision to join (or remain in) the Church. Who has supported your growth as a Christian? Did you ever take a break from it? If you took a break, how did you return? What/who was helpful? What does it feel like to renew your baptismal covenant? What were your experiences of baptism and confirmation like? What was wonderful? Telling? Puzzling? Do you find them odd? Strangely solemn and special or simple and trivial? What do they say to you about family and community? About personal transformation and new life?

Unless you remember your baptism, you may well be tempted to think you were always a Christian. But as Tertullian said in the third century, "Christians are made, not born."[1] This is true, in part, because *God cannot make us Christians against our will.* You may want to recall the process by which you became, consciously and freely, a Christian. Again, you may want to jot some ideas down.

Baptism in the early Church. In order to explore the meanings of baptism it is a good idea to also begin with its earliest forms, to avoid the trap of thinking that early Christian baptisms were a short, sweet rite done semi-privately with family and friends. They were a whole community affair, major, solemn, and therefore, in the best sense of *significant,* full of meaning.

Baptism made you a member of the Christian community after an extended period of preparation, followed by a free choice to join it. Soon, and in order to fully include children in the eucharist, we began to baptize infants. Theologically, however, the baptism of babies is an *exception* to the norm of a conscious preparation followed by a conscious decision to follow Christ as a member of his Body, the Church.

By "norm," liturgical scholars do not mean "what most people do," but the theological standard of celebration of a sacrament *in its fullness.* From this we make adaptations, exceptions, and so forth, such as

1 Tertullian, *Apologeticus pro Cristianis,* xviii.

the baptism of infants, for it is cruel to have children in the assembly and not fully include them as full members. That is why we baptize them, riding, as it were, on their parents' and godparents' faith and commitment to raise them as Christians. It makes little sense, therefore, to baptize infants of parents who are not committed to doing so.

Early Christians did not baptize easily. The Church was not understood to be anything like a spiritual self-service store, but rather an extended family, a household, a community, a city—even a nation. We understood that one does not become a member of a community overnight without *a process of belonging.* Therefore candidates went through a gradual exploration of the Christian life in community before they were asked to make a commitment to Christ and his Church. This process of preparation led to a final, intense preparation during Lent if baptism was to take place at Easter. Many parishes are returning to this practice, especially as increasing numbers of adults come to us as seekers without any prior acquaintance with Christianity. They have a right to explore life with us before they make a commitment.

Lent originated as a period of imitation of Christ facing temptations of the Accuser (Satan) in the desert, and of preparation for those who would be baptized either just before or at Easter. Throughout, candidates fasted, gave alms, and most importantly, explored how their lives and behaviors were being transformed by the Good News of the nearness of God's reign of justice, peace, and love. Hearing the Good News, the candidates for baptism were encouraged to examine their lives and make decisions to change in ways small or large. This process of change or transformation is what the Greek term *metanoia*—translated as "conversion" and "repentance"—actually means: a *turning or change of heart*, much more than only an intellectual assent to doctrinal statements or a feeling of remorse and compunction.

How does this apply to you? If you were baptized as an infant, you probably have had to consciously decide for yourself at some point(s) whether you wish to be a member of the Christian community, and in many ways, you probably went through a process somewhat similar to the process an adult went through on the way to becoming a member of the Church. You may well find parallels to your experience in the following description of this ancient process of preparation for baptism.

Journey to new life. God has been known to use almost anything—even awful experiences like divorce or bereavement—to call us lovingly to a deeper awareness of our share in the divine life. Recalling what first made you *consciously* interested in exploring (or reaffirming) the Christian way of life might bring along some surprises. See how the following pattern applies to you—or not:

First contact. Most of the time we are not aware of our connection to God—indeed we can go on for decades without noticing it. But just because we are not aware does not mean that God is not there. Whether through the example of a Christian in the workplace, or perhaps an interior sense that there is more to life than shopping, or through a difficult period of loss, the earliest Christians (and you?) heard good news: "God's loving reign is coming: turn your hearts and trust this Good News."[2] Whether you would have put it this way is unimportant. They—and you?—approached the Christian community and inquired. We (yes, me too) found welcome, acceptance, and trust, as well as hard work on behalf of the poor and marginalized. After a period of getting acquainted, the ancient seeker signed on as a student to further explore this way of living.

Developing Christian skills. Being a Christian does not come naturally. Any two-year-old will tell you that being of the side of the underdog is crazy, and that the biggest cookie is, of course, *for him.* Additionally, Christianity is not a theory, or a bundle of philosophical convictions, but a *way* to be in the world. This way involves four basic skills: being able to read and interpret the Bible for yourself, in a ma-

---

2 This is the meaning of the word "gospel" (*euangelion*) and its cognates: evangel, evangelism, evangelization, and so forth; that is, the proclamation of the Good News of the nearness of God's reign of justice, peace, and love. Cf. Mark 1:–15.

ture, responsible way; being able to participate fully and consciously in worship, finding in it both *your* meanings and *ours* crafted over centuries; being able to develop and be responsible for your own spiritual life and prayer habits; and finally, being able to willingly serve those in need, especially the poor.

In the early Church a student of the Christian way—let's call her Sally—engaged in all four of these skills from the beginning, learning as she went, week by week. It began well before Lent, and took several months at least, maybe a year or even more. Little by little, as God's Word resounded in Sally's ear and heart (the root meaning of "catechumen"), she began to try tiny or major new behaviors in response to God's love. The day came when she began to say, "I used to. . . but now I. . . "—her heart was slowly transforming. Along with this came an increasing ability to trust herself, God, and others, and a growing sense of peace. Lent approached, and on its first Sunday, the congregation agreed to Sally's baptism, where she would be fully incorporated into the community.

Lent was the right time to do something natural at this stage: to name the behaviors, people, habits, and decisions that kept her away from God, and with the help of sponsors and teachers, to learn to leave these behind. In the process, we also shared the creed Sally would profess in her baptism, and the Lord's Prayer.

Baptism in the early Church. Finally the big day arrived. After fasting on the previous day, Sally and her sponsors arrived at the church gathering, and were led to water—a stream or river, perhaps a lake, and later, a building separate from the basilica, housing a large pool of water. She took off her clothes.

Stripping. Baptism took place stark naked. Men and women were baptized separately, the women baptized by women deacons, and then all confirmed immediately after by the priest—later, the bishop. Before any of this took place, however, their clothes had to come off. Stripping expressed all the things the candidates were leaving behind as a result of their change of heart. As Bishop Cyril of Jerusalem put it,

> As soon, then, as you entered, you put off your tunic; and this was an image of putting off the old person with her deeds. Having stripped yourselves, you were naked; in this also imitating Christ, who was stripped naked on the Cross, and by His nakedness put off from Himself the principalities and powers, and openly triumphed over them on the tree. . . O wondrous thing! You were naked in the sight of all, and were not ashamed; for truly you bore

the likeness of the first-formed Adam,
who was naked in the garden, and was
not ashamed.[3]

Profession of faith. Sally then professed the faith of
the apostles in God the Creator of all things, in Jesus,
who was enfleshed in Mary, died, was buried, and
rose again; in the Holy Spirit, the universal ("catholic") Church, which is the communion of saints,
in the forgiven-ness of sins,[4] the resurrection of the
body and eternal life.[5]

In Jerusalem, the candidate was then rubbed with
exorcised oil to be rid of evil:

> Then. . . you were anointed with exor-
> cised oil, from the very hairs of your
> head to your feet, and were made par-
> takers of the good olive-tree, Jesus
> Christ. For you were cut off from the
> wild olive-tree, and grafted into the
> good one, and were made to share the
> fatness of the true olive-tree.[6]

---

3 Cyril of Jerusalem, Catecheses, 20.

4 *Forgiven-ness*: Not forgiveness *if* you. . . , but sins *already* forgiven, just as Jesus's proclamation claimed. See the section on
   confession in the following chapter.

5 Literally, "the life of the Age" of God's reign of justice, peace, and
   love, begun with Jesus's resurrection.

6 Cyril of Jerusalem, Catecheses, 20..

Immersion. The candidate waded into the water, and either knelt and bowed into it three times, or, if standing in shallow water, a copious amount was poured over her three times in the name of the Father, the Son, and the Holy Spirit. Bishop Cyril wrote,

> After these things, you were led to the holy pool of Divine Baptism, as Christ was carried from the Cross to the Sepulchre which is before our eyes. [an indication that this was delivered in the *Anastasis* rotunda at the Holy Sepulcher]. And each of you was asked, whether he believed in the name of the Father, and of the Son, and of the Holy Ghost, . . . and descended three times into the water, and ascended again; here also hinting by a symbol at the three days burial of Christ. . . at the self-same moment you were both dying and being born; and that water of salvation was at once your grave and your mother.[7]

Anointing with chrism. The candidate rose from the water and was anointed from head to toe with chrism—perfumed olive oil consecrated by the bishop. In the Old Testament, chrism was used to anoint

---

7 Cyril of Jerusalem, *ibid.*

kings and prophets as a sign of being chosen by God. By anointing Sally, we proclaimed her royalty as a member of the Christian community, a "...chosen kindred, a royal priesthood, a holy nation" (1 Peter 2:9). Imagine a Roman slave being anointed as royalty at her baptism!

"You are sealed by the Holy Spirit in Baptism and marked as Christ's own for ever," says the bishop or priest to the newly baptized as a cross is etched on their foreheads glistening with oil.[8] According to Basil the Great, in baptism we come alive in the Spirit:

> . . . the water receiving the body as in a tomb figures [symbolizes] death, while the Spirit pours in the quickening power, renewing our souls from the deadness of sin unto their original life. This then is what it is to be born again of water and of the Spirit, the being made dead being effected in the water, while our life is wrought in us through the Spirit.[9]

We will be exploring the Holy Spirit in more detail in the final chapter of the book, but here I should point out that in the Episcopal Church, a baptized

8 BCP, 308.
9 Basil the Great, *On the Holy Spirit*, 15.

person fully receives the gift of God's own Spirit in *baptism.*

Anointing, that is, rubbing with oil, at baptism varied greatly from East to West in the early Church. Anointing is mentioned first *metaphorically* to refer to being "anointed" by the "spirit of gladness," the Holy Spirit. At least until the late third century, we were "anointed" with the *Spirit* rather than oil. So it was probably not until the late third century that the Greco-Roman custom of rubbing the whole body with oil before and/or after bathing (found also in the Old Testament) became an *illustration* of the anointing by the Spirit. Later, by the fifth century, the descent of the Spirit became associated specifically with the anointing with oil.

It varied. Eventually, as the practice continued to develop in the West, we ended up with two anointings: one after the bath, and one at the end of the service of baptism, on the head only, done by the bishop.

Dressing and Enlightenment. Once dried, the baptized were dressed in a gown—usually white—or in new clothing (customs varied). By the fourth century a lit candle was given to the neophyte as a sign of purity and enlightenment, and indeed, sometimes baptism was referred to as enlightenment.

Imagine yourself at the Lateran Baptistery, a separate, much smaller building next to the basilica in Rome, containing an octagonal pool about three feet deep. It is the Easter Vigil, and the bishop, call him Theodore, has finished the prayer over those just immersed who stand before him. The water rite has ended. Meanwhile, the rest of the congregation has been waiting in the basilica praying while the immersions went on. Before they leave the baptistry, Theodore "consigns"—that is, seals with a cross, the way a signet ring seals an imprint on wax—the glistening foreheads of the newly baptized, and lays his hands on them, as a final blessing. This laying on of hands, or *missa* (sending), often ended services.[10] The new Christians are thus born not only to the new life of grace, but are sent to join a new family, the Christian community, the Church. They file out into the basilica, to the riotous applause of the waiting congregation. Some try to touch them still gleaming with oil, putting some of it on themselves. The eucharist proceeds with the Prayers of the People and the procession of gifts.

This second anointing and laying on of hands later drifted away from the baptismal rite and became a separate event, "confirmation." The story is quite a cautionary tale:

Origins of "Confirmation." There is evidence that some bishops in southern France who could not be at all baptisms were consigning baptized Christians

---

10 As early as 416 CE Pope Innocent I explained this as the Roman custom in his *Letter to Decentius of Gubbio* (PL 20, 550–552).

at some other time afterward as early as the fifth or sixth century. By the ninth century, though, a request from Emperor Charlemagne in Germany arrived in Rome, asking for the Roman liturgical books, as he intended to unify the worship of his kingdom. The bishop of Rome was Hadrian I. So the books of the bishop of Rome were sent north. But in the North (Aachen), Christianization had proceeded much more slowly, and unlike the Mediterranean cities, which had a bishop in every town, priests could of course carry out the baptismal rite, but the consignation with laying on of hands had to be done when a bishop came around. Thus confirmation developed as a separate rite in the West. In the Eastern Churches this problem never surfaced, and to this day, the baptizing priest also anoints and lays hands on the baptized (that is, "confirms") them *within* the rite of baptism, in a single, integrated rite of incorporation. Moral of the story: do not make an exception, due to circumstances, into a norm!

In the Episcopal Church's BCP 1979 "confirmation" appears among the *pastoral* offices, along with reception and reaffirmation, indicating that we do not consider confirmation a rite of incorporation into Christ and his Church, since baptism constitutes full and complete membership.[11] In our theology, confirmation is understood rather as a "mature

---

11 BCP, 298.

public affirmation of their faith,"[12] and so it is becoming more common to see confirmands of a later
age—persons who have had the time and interest to
explore the Christian life and faith and freely make
the decision they could not make at their infant
baptisms. Should confirmation ever go back to the
baptism rite where it originated, we will still need a
mature affirmation of faith, as well as a new rite of
passage for adolescents.

Additionally, experiencing confirmation as a separate rite often runs the risk of attaching to it meanings that simply are not there. A close look at the rite
of confirmation will show that it does not mention
becoming an Episcopalian. Though an individual
baptized in a different denomination may *experience*
this rite as one of incorporation into the Episcopal
Church, the rite does not say so, for it is simply a
mature affirmation of *baptismal* faith. The rite that
actually expresses this transition is the rite of reception, generally celebrated with those who were baptized *and confirmed* in a different denomination.

Should confirmation return once again to its original place within the sacrament of baptism, as the
Orthodox have it to this day? In spite of thorough
research, the restoration of the full process of preparation for baptism (catechumenate) and the desire
of the drafters of the BCP 1979 to do so, reluctance

---

12 BCP, 412.

apparently continues, due both to our fascination with bishops and the association of confirmation with adolescence,[13] in spite of the original intent of the writers of the BCP 1979, thwarted by the General Convention that approved it.

Opening the treasure. In the fourth century Sally would have worn her white baptismal robe during all of the following week. And during the seven weeks of Easter, she would have attended more classes! This time, the bishop would "open up" the meaning of what the recently baptized had experienced. So Cyril of Jerusalem, for example, began his talks by saying,

> Since I well knew that seeing is far more persuasive than hearing, I waited till now, so that you would be open to my words from your *experience,* and I might lead you by the hand into the brighter and more fragrant meadow of the Paradise before us; for you have received the more sacred Mysteries, after having been found worthy of divine and life-giving Baptism.[14]

So the new Christians did not end their process of transformation with their baptisms. They continued

---

13 Cf. Paul Turner, "Between Consultation and Faithfulness: Questions That Won't Go Away," *Worship,* 89/4 (July 2015), 351–358.

14 Cyril of Jerusalem, *Catechetical Lectures,* 19, emphasis mine.

to meet for seven weeks after to learn and reflect upon the meaning of the sacraments they had experienced. Today, where the art of teaching is a bit more developed, it is best to engage the newly baptized in a process of reflecting together on their experience of baptism and eucharist by gathering them with their sponsors (and parents) and anyone in the congregation that wishes to observe, to watch a video of the rite as one asks, "What was that like for you? What does it mean for you?" It is often amazing how people with no formal education in theology express ancient understandings as their own. In a sense, that is precisely what this book attempts to do: to engage you in thinking about your experience of worship, in conversation with the tradition of the Church.

The meanings of baptism. Bathing as a ritual practice is extremely common among world religions. Christian baptism (the word means immersing or dipping) originated as a Jewish rite of purification and renewal. Still today, pious Jews immerse themselves in a *mikvah,* or pool of water, as a sign of repentance, purification, and new beginnings. It is also a required part of the process of converting to Judaism, along with circumcision if one is male. About the meaning of Jewish baptism, Rabbi Maurice Lamm writes,

> Jewish tradition prescribes a profound symbol. It instructs the conversion can-

didate to place himself or herself in a radically different physical environment—in water rather than air. This leaves the person floating—momentarily suspended without breathing—substituting the usual forward moving nature and purposeful stride that characterize his or her waking movements with an aimlessness, a weightlessness, a detachment from the former environment. Individuality, passion, ego—all are submerged in the metamorphosis from the larval state of the present to a new existence.[15]

The baptism of Jesus. There are several prisms through which we can understand the meanings of Christian baptism. One of them, perhaps the earliest, is Jesus's own experience of it. The Gospel according to Mark describes it in chapter one:

And in those days it happened that Jesus, from Nazareth of Galilee came and was baptized in the Jordan by John. And immediately rising up out of the water, he saw the heavens being rent apart

15 Rabbi Maurice Lamm, "The Mikveh's Significance in Traditional Conversion," https://www.myjewishlearning.com/article/why-immerse-in-the-mikveh/, accessed 7/17/19.

and the Spirit descending on him like
a dove. And a voice out of the heavens:
"You are my Son, the beloved, in you I
have delighted.

Mark 1:9–11

A friend once described her experience of baptism at age ten. She recalled how she felt celebrated, loved, regarded. It was an experience similar to
hearing, "You are my daughter, the beloved, in you
I have delighted." *All of us, without exception,* can
hear these words from God as applied to ourselves.
This is not to say that we are sons and daughters of
God in the same way as Jesus ("eternally begotten
of the Father, God from God, Light from Light, true
God from true God, . . . of one Being with the Father"),[16] but we—and all creation with us—are God's
children in whom God is well pleased. God says to
each of us deep down in the core of our selves, "You
are my child, I love you, I am proud of you." Like
the Baptism of Jesus, ours *reveals* who we truly are:
beloved daughters and sons of God.

Conversion and forgiveness. Another prism for the
meaning of baptism is conversion or change of
heart, for it acknowledges and proclaims the forgiven-ness of sins. David Bentley Hart, in his recent
literal translation of the New Testament, points out

---

16 BCP, 327.

that wherever the term appears that we translate as "forgiveness," it should rather be translated as "for-giveN-Ness." This is for two reasons: first, the example of Jesus in the gospels shows him declaring forgiven-ness to sinners freely and without any conditions, not even repentance. Second, because in the theology of St. Paul, Christ's death on the cross was the price paid to free us from enslavement to sin, erasing all sins. So another layer of meaning in baptism is the proclamation that we have *already* been forgiven, not that we *will be* forgiven given certain conditions.

Jesus's Passover and our own: The other prism through which we understand baptism is Jesus's own baptism in blood—his death and new life. Thus the new, Christian, understanding of baptism is not only that it is a sign of conversion and a new beginning as in Judaism, but of our being beloved children of God, already forgiven, and joined to Christ through an imitation of his death, in his new, risen, life. An imitation. A *likeness*. Baptism is a *sign* that is *alike* to Christ's death. Bishop Cyril, for example, wrote,

> . . . fix your mind with much attention on the words of the Apostle [Paul]. He said not, For if we have been planted together with His death, but, with the *likeness* of His death. For in Christ's case there was death in reality, for His soul was re-

ally separated from His body, and real burial, for His holy body was wrapped in pure linen; and everything happened really to Him; but in your case there was only a likeness of death and sufferings, whereas of salvation [healing and safekeeping] there was not a likeness but a reality.[17]

Regeneration or rebirth. Baptism is also a form of spiritual rebirth. As early as the writing of the gospel according to John, we find an allusion to it in the story about Nicodemus coming to see Jesus by night. Jesus tells him, a Jewish leader, "Amen, amen, I tell you, unless a person is born of water and spirit, he cannot enter the reign of God" (John 3:3–5). Baptism is in this sense, a new birth, enlightening us to see a spiritual reality already underway: the Reign of God.

The gift of the Spirit. Finally, another prism through which the meaning of baptism is manifest is the gift of the Holy Spirit. In baptism we are not only made one with Christ, but receive the third person of the Trinity, the Holy Spirit. This means that we are connected through both the Word and the Spirit, to the Father, or Source of all that is, and are therefore brought into the life of God, a community of three different Persons united in love and joy, of equal dignity

---

17 Cyril of Jerusalem, *Catechetical Lectures*, 20.

and divinity. The presence of the Holy Spirit brings with it several aspects: *wisdom,* true knowledge born of experience; *understanding,* discerning what God is up to in our lives according in the light of Scripture; *knowledge,* or the ability to think and reflect upon our experience of faith in God's self-revelation; *counsel,* or being able to recognize God's will and make decisions congruent with it; *fortitude,* the courage to do what is right even at great risk; *piety,* or devotion to God; and *fear of the Lord,* that is, amazement or awe before God, the cause of all that is.

The meaning of confirmation. If being "buried" in a pool (exactly like the Jewish custom) is a sign of all these things, what is signified by the laying on of hands in baptism or later, in "confirmation"?

The laying on of hands as a ritual gesture also has a long Jewish history, associated with authorization, delegation, giving (or recognizing) the Spirit, and so forth, and continued likewise in the New Testament. In the context of baptism, the bishop blessed and sent the baptized to the gathered congregation in a single gesture. The laying on of hands was interpreted *later* as sealing with the Spirit since it accompanied consignation with chrism, but as we have seen, it was the baptism itself that was considered the seal (imprint) of the Spirit in the earliest traditions.

Through the laying on of hands we are, in a sense, deputized and sent as a limb of Christ's Body into the world. It is not surprising that the same gesture is the core of the ordination rites, for baptism is our ordination into the order of the laity—the source and warrant of all lay ministry and authority. We will explore this more fully in chapter five, when we look at ordination.

What a profound experience this full rite of incorporation as a member must have been for Sally! Here, in one coherent Jewish ritual reinterpreted in a Christian way and imitating Christ's own dying and rising, the process through which they had been going is expressed in physical and emotional, as well as intellectual and spiritual, ways. Again, Tertullian:

> The flesh is washed, in order that the soul may be cleansed; the flesh is anointed, that the soul may be consecrated; the flesh is signed [with the cross], that the soul too may be fortified; the flesh is shadowed with the imposition of hands, that the soul also may be illuminated by the Spirit; the flesh feeds on the body and blood of Christ, that the soul likewise may fatten on its God.[18]

18 Tertullian, *On the Resurrection of the flesh*, VIII.

Here, in the norm of baptism as a full rite, "conversion" is not only a matter of assenting to ideas and creeds. It is also a deeply meaningful expression of candidates' transformation over time, *metanoia*—an experience dramatically enacted in a rich ritual action forming and informing the rest of the candidates' lives, while also birthing and shaping the Christian community, who see themselves and their own baptisms in the new Christians coming out of the water.

Getting in touch with your baptism. How might we get in touch with such a rich understanding of the core event that makes us Christians if we cannot remember it? There are two major ways:

It is helpful to celebrate baptisms as fully and richly as possible, and as close to the norm, not only with a full and complete use of symbols in abundance, but after a generous period of preparation of the candidates (or their parents) and godparents and to schedule the rite on a major Sunday, before the whole congregation, following it with a period of reflection on what has taken place.

Additionally, at Easter and also whenever someone is baptized, the whole congregation reaffirms our baptismal covenant. For those who have been away from the Church for some time, and anyone joining the Episcopal Church in confirmation or reception, these may be profoundly meaningful experiences.

They too deserve the same process of preparation for the rite and reflection upon it afterward.

Conclusion. Holy Baptism and confirmation reveal that we are in fact children of God, in whom God is well pleased, and are together both a sign of a change of heart, of dying and rising, of forgiveness, of new birth and new beginnings, and of being royalty, sent with authority. By imitating his death, baptism and confirmation together intimately join us to Christ's body, as "living members of the Body of your Son, and heirs of your eternal kingdom."[19] This is why, when the priest says, "the Body of Christ" at communion, she is not talking about the bread only, but about you as well.

> O strange and inconceivable thing! We did not really die, we were not really buried, we were not really crucified and raised again; *but our imitation was in a figure, and our healing in reality.* Christ was actually crucified, and actually buried, and truly rose again; and all these things He has freely bestowed upon us, that we, sharing His sufferings by imitation, might gain salvation in reality. O surpassing loving-kindness! Christ re-

---

19 BCP, 366.

ceived nails in His undefiled hands and feet, and suffered anguish; while on me without pain or toil by the fellowship of His suffering He freely bestows healing.[20]

---

20 Cyril of Jerusalem, *Catechetical Lectures*, 20, 5, emphasis mine.

Chapter IV

Talking and Eating with God

The Eucharist

Immediately after their baptisms, the new members joined the Christian community in the celebration of the *eucharist*, or thanksgiving. We will explore it in its two parts: the Word of God and the Holy Communion, reviewing first what we do and its history, and then the meanings we have found in them, action by action.

Your experience. What has been your experience of participating in the eucharist? Life-giving? Restoring? Forgiving? Enraging? Frustrating? Incomprehensible? Boring? What has been wonderful, and what has been a challenge? What is it like for you to gather with other Christians every Sunday—or most Sundays? If your congregation at eucharist were to magically disappear, what would be lost to *you*?

The first part of our gathering was, and still is, the Word of God. At eucharists, we gather together—and with God. In fact, the Greek word *ekklesia*, translated in English as "church," actually means "assembly." It originally referred to an assembly of elected Greek officials called together to deliberate, like our legislatures. The Church was understood to be an assembly elected (literally, "called out") and convened by God. Your local church is an *assembly of people*, regardless of where you gather, whether at the church's building or at a picnic eucharist in the woods. There are four significant actions that the assembly always carries out in this part of the eucharist: gathering, listening, sharing, and praying. Before we examine each in its own right, it will be helpful to review the earliest eucharists and what they looked like.

The earliest eucharists. Meals feature often in the New Testament, indicating that even before we developed rich theological understandings of the event, we simply got together to share a meal. Even then, though, Jesus's practice of eating with the wrong people had a specific meaning as a *sign,* as we shall see below.

Imagine yourself a follower of the Way (the first name we gave ourselves, before "Christian"), in the bustling city of Corinth, around the year 53 CE. You and members of your household gather with others in the large home of a well-to-do member. There are perhaps between thirty and fifty people there. Normally you would bring something for the potluck, but today all the food is provided by the host. You are not surprised by the presence of homeless people, slaves and free people, men and women, Roman citizens and foreigners, together. The meal is a radically egalitarian event in a culture in which it was extremely important to eat with the right people and avoid the wrong ones. The menu is probably mostly bread and vegetables, though perhaps it also included fish. Meat was probably avoided since it was associated with sacrifices to the gods in pagan temples.

Shared meals like these gradually began to take place either Saturday after sundown or early on Sunday morning, before work, and were associated with "the Day of the Lord," that is, the day of Christ's resurrection but also the day of the fulfillment of the reign (kingdom) of God, here on earth.

These gatherings did not take place in churches initially but in homes, whether the home of members wealthy enough to accommodate a large group, or modest homes and apartments—even shops—where a smaller group might meet. As the assemblies grew in size, homes were remodeled and enlarged to suit those purposes.

By 150 CE, in a Syrian community in Rome, the event had developed its basic structure, which we observe to this day: we gathered, heard God's Word, shared its meaning, prayed for Church and world, gave thanks to God, ate together, and were sent out. Let's look at the first four actions: gathering, listening, sharing, and praying.

We gather. Justin the Martyr, a layman writing to the emperor Antoninus Pius around 150 CE, described what we did on Sundays in that Syrian community in Rome:

And on the day called Sunday, all who live in cities or in the country gather together to one place, and the memoirs of the apostles or the writings of the prophets are read, as long as time permits; then, when the reader has ceased, the president verbally instructs, and exhorts to the imitation of these good things. Then we all rise together and pray. . . [1]

Our first significant action in the eucharist, then, is *gathering*. This begins the minute you leave home, but it comes to its climax as the Church comes together, singing a song of praise, and ending with our prayers "collected" in a *collect* said by the one who presides. This gathering rite may be extended by adding an *optional* entrance hymn and prayer for purification, but nevertheless the core of the action is an acclamation, a hymn, and prayer.

In this sense at least, simply gathering in the name of Christ already is a sign, as found in that earliest Church order, the *Didache*, or Teaching, whose Eucharistic Prayer asks God, ". . . may your Church be gathered together from the ends of the earth unto your kingdom."[2]

---

1   Justin Martyr, *Apologia*, 67.
2   Didache 9:4. Translation mine.

From the very beginning of the eucharistic gathering, we are reminded that we are, already, in God's
reign (kingdom). What does gathering mean? And *to
whom*? Here is what it meant to the great Orthodox
theologian Alexander Schmemann:

> The liturgy of the Eucharist is best under-
> stood as a journey or procession. It is the
> journey of the Church into the dimension
> of the Kingdom. We use the word "dimen-
> sion" because it seems the best way to in-
> dicate the manner of our sacramental en-
> trance into the risen life of Christ. Color
> transparencies "come alive" when viewed
> in three dimensions instead of two. The
> presence of the added dimension allows
> us to see much better the actual reality
> of what has been photographed. In very
> much the same way, though of course
> any analogy is condemned to fail, our en-
> trance into the presence of Christ is an
> entrance into a fourth dimension which
> allows us to see the ultimate reality of
> life. It is not an escape from the world,
> rather it is the arrival at a vantage point
> from which we can see more deeply into
> the reality of the world.[3]

3 Alexander Schmemann, *For the Life of the World: Sacraments and
   Orthodoxy* (Crestwood, NY: St. Vladimir's Seminary Press, 2004), 3.

We listen to God's Word. Once we are gathered, we hear God's Word. Two biblical readings are proclaimed: one from the Old Testament or Acts, a second reading from the New Testament. The first and second readings may be followed by a psalm or a hymn. Finally, we hear a reading from the gospels. This reading may be honored in special ways: the book may be carried in procession accompanied by imperial Roman signs of honor like lights and incense, or simply proclaimed from the same pulpit or lectern as the other readings.

Throughout, we are listening to God's Word, that is, God's message to us here, today. We do this through texts originally written in foreign languages thousands of years ago, and addressed to a very different people. It is important to understand their historical, cultural, linguistic, and even socioeconomic context, or we may seriously distort the texts, projecting meanings that were not there originally. Understanding the texts in their context, we can then find parallel meanings in our *own context*. Since biblical texts were originally written in Hebrew and Greek, this is a good place to say a word about translation.

Translation is an art. It is carried out by professionals, who, at least bilingual, always translate *into their first language,* whose rhythms and nuances they carry, as it were, in their blood. It cannot be done well by a machine, for, more often than not, there are no exact correspondences from language to language, but what is said in one language finds *similar or analogous* expressions in another, not literally the same. For this reason alone it is wise for proclaimers of the Word at worship to consult more than one translation as they prepare. Throughout this book I am using David Bentley Hart's new translation of the New Testament for it is as literal as possible—and therefore at times ungrammatical, inelegant, and inappropriate for liturgical use; it offers, however, the meaning of a text in its original context, so the reader may find the analogous meanings in theirs. It is also very helpful to the average congregant to *hear* rather than read the Word proclaimed, for in hearing it, the text takes on a life and surprising relevance all its own, opening new avenues of interpretation every single time, allowing us to encounter it afresh.

What does listening to God together as a community mean? We gather to listen, so it is immediately evident that the Speaker has something to say that we *value*. It may be shocking, surprising, consoling, revolutionary, life-changing, or predictable, but the very act of proclamation assumes that it is something worth listening to—something for which we are grateful—so we respond, "thanks be to God." This means perhaps that the meaning of being here, alive, comes from a Source beyond ourselves, just as we do not create ourselves either.

Sharing the meanings of the texts. Listening to God's Word would be a lot easier if God spoke univocally, every sentence crystal clear, with scientific exactness, leaving no room for interpretation. But God respects us too much for that, and knowing that the Word must be meaningful to each of us in our particularity, the Speaker speaks in parables, metaphors, stories, and other poetic ways, which we must interpret for ourselves here and now. To be able to engage in this, the operative question is, What does this message mean to me/us in my/our life today?

Even with the best translations, the task of applying the Word to our local, immediate situation requires work. This usually takes place in the form of a sermon or homily, in which the preacher "opens up" the Word proclaimed, exploring its meanings for us today. It can also take place when a group of Christians simply share what the Word means to them in their context, as we do in such exercises as *lectio divina* and African Bible Reflection sessions during preparation for baptism, confirmation, and so forth, where the participants share what the passage means to them. Sometimes in small congregations, the *Lectio Divina* method or African Bible Reflection may be used in place of a sermon, or in response to it.

Too often we can hear and interpret the Word only as it affects each of us in our individual lives, and the meaning of the Word to the congregation or parish community remains unexplored. Preachers can, and should, seek to articulate what God is telling not only individuals but the community as a whole.

The Creed. For almost a thousand years, most of Western Christianity managed to celebrate the eucharist without the Nicene Creed. Promulgated by the bishops gathered by Constantine at Nicea in 325, and expanded in Constantinople in 381 CE, this Creed was developed to expel the Arians from the assembly, for they believed that the second person of the Trinity is a creature of God, unequal to the Father. In the East the Creed was added to the eucharist as early as 511 CE, but in the West it was included only in Spain in 589; there, the invasion of the Arian Visigoths made them particular targets of the accusation of heresy. It was only in the early eleventh century that the Western Church included it in the eucharist everywhere.

An entire book could be written on the issue of whether the Nicene Creed belongs in the eucharist at all. Here I would only point out several details: First, the original context and purpose of the Nicene Creed was to exclude the Arians. Additionally, its philosophical language, to be crystal clear, is different from the usual metaphorical, poetic style employed in worship. Moreover, for a thousand years the Great Thanksgiving was, and continues to be, our main creedal statement in the eucharist, to which we assent with our final *Amen*, required for it to be valid. Finally, it seems that our Eucharistic Prayer B's progression of ideas may have been influenced by the Apostle's (or baptismal) Creed, which

forms the core of the Nicene-Constantinopolitan
Creed as well. The baptismal or Apostle's Creed,
which preceded it, *was* essential in baptism. Such
baptismal creeds are much older than the Nicene.
So we cannot say that reciting the Creed is essential to the eucharist—in the Holy Eucharist Rite II it
must only be recited on Sundays and major feasts.[4]

We pray for the Church and the world. Now that we
have heard of God's love and intention for of all creation, we dare speak up and say "help!" As Justin the
Martyr described it,

> "[we] offer hearty prayers in common
> for ourselves and for the baptized per-
> son, [he is talking about a eucharist
> following a baptism] and for all others
> in every place, that we may be counted
> worthy, now that we have learned the
> truth, by our works also to be found
> good citizens and keepers of the com-
> mandments, so that we may be saved
> with an everlasting salvation."

The prayer book instructs us to do so:

---

4 BCP, 358.

> Prayer is offered with intercession for
> The Universal Church, its members,
>   and its mission
> The Nation and all in authority
> The welfare of the world
> The concerns of the local community
> Those who suffer and those
>   in any trouble
> The departed (with commemoration
>   of a saint when appropriate)[5]

Since in rubrics the first instance is always the preferred form, we should note that the rubric first directs the congregation to pray for several categories of concern. *If* the congregation cannot do this the forms provided by the prayer book may be employed. The rubric prefers that the congregation voice their own prayers, either spontaneously or employing locally crafted forms.

It is in the light of God's Word that we speak up, interceding for the Church and the world. Who are we to intercede for Church and world? The First Letter of Peter succinctly explains,

> . . . you are a chosen kindred, a royal
> priesthood, a holy nation, a people held
> in peculiar possession so that you may

5 BCP, 383.

openly proclaim the virtues of the one
who called you out of darkness into his
wondrous light.

1 Peter 2:9

As a royal priesthood, we *all*, not only clergy, offer prayers to God, interceding for the needs of the
Church and the world. This is an especially powerful moment whenever the Prayers of the People are
crafted locally to reflect local needs, which often express wider needs of the whole world. Additionally,
our prayers for the Church and world are, in a way,
the agenda for our witnessing and service. Perhaps
this is why traditionally they were led by deacons,
ordained to bring the needs of the world to the attention of the Church. At the very least deacons
should listen to what the people are praying for, and
organize the congregation to address these needs in
their locality. More about that later, as we explore
the orders of the Church.

Some congregations insert prayers for birthdays,
anniversaries, and so forth at some point between
the Word and the Table. These are best included in
the Prayers of the People, before the final collect.

In the second century, the eucharist described
by Justin Martyr continued with the Peace and the
Great Thanksgiving, but five hundred years ago we
inserted the Confession.

The Confession. We confess our sins and receive absolution. This is another relatively recent development, in a history spanning two millennia. The Protestant Reformers, after doing away with private confession and absolution, introduced the people's confession in the eucharist to encourage reception of communion, as people had been unaccustomed for almost a thousand years to receiving it. Rome quickly followed suit. Thus seen in the historical development of the eucharist, the confession and absolution are neither theologically nor historically essential to the eucharist, and may be omitted "on occasion."[6] But what does it mean to confess and be absolved?

"Oh, Juan, why do we have to keep mentioning sin?" wailed an aging hippie one Sunday. "Hmm; what does it mean to you?" I shot back in a flash of good pastoring. "Well," he said, "Sin is something *so awful that it cannot be forgiven.*" There, in that innocent reply, lies a serious misunderstanding of the Christian faith and God's love and mercy. The two reasons why we talk about sin are: it is real, and *it has been forgiven. Yes, already.*

Sin is real, even though the Anglo Saxon *synne* is not a very good translation of the original Greek *hamartia*, a term from archery meaning *missing the mark*—an error, a mistake, a lapse. The Latin term *peccatum* implies tripping, faltering, or stumbling.

---

6 BCP, 359.

So *synne* (related to the root for "crime") seems a bit strong, at least most of the time. Yet we recognize that we all make mistakes, bad choices, and errors; that we falter, lapse, trip, and stumble, all the time, sometimes in minor ways, sometimes spectacularly, hurting others, ourselves, our planet. It's part of being human.

And *God has already forgiven it*, as Jesus's own practice of forgiveness shows in the gospels. He would tell people that their sins were forgiven, *without condition.* No repentance needed, nothing more than a sense of "this guy can help me." That, he called faith *(pistis)*, meaning something closer to *faithful allegiance.* Only after declaring forgiveness did he *sometimes* say, "Don't do it again." It must have made the temple scribes and priests livid. He was destroying their livelihood, removing the need to pay for and earn forgiveness from God through religious offerings. It may have cost Jesus his life.

Interpreting meaning of the death of Jesus theologically, Paul, writing in Romans, pointed to Jesus's death as *God's* payment *of the price of our freedom from slavery* to the powers of evil and death, reconciling us: "But God shows his own love to us in that, while we were yet sinners, the Anointed [Christ] died on our behalf" (Romans 5:8).[7] Forgiveness is

---

7 The popular misconception that Jesus died to pay *God* for our sins is based on a misreading of the Letter to the Romans. What Paul wrote is that through his own Son's sacrifice, *God* was paying the price of our emancipation from slavery to the powers of evil, sin, and death.

God's way of reconciling with us, present through all of Jesus's life, even on the cross. It is accomplished *already*. We cannot make it happen by manipulating God, for it is a free gift. Perhaps this is why participation in the eucharist without confession was the norm during the early centuries. As Ephrem the Syrian put it,

> . . . whoever eats in belief the Bread made holy in My name, if he be pure, he will be preserved in his purity; and if he be a sinner, he will be forgiven.[8]

So if we mention sin it is because it is forgiven, and not to impute guilt and stand in judgment of others. In our communal confession we are not earning forgiveness by feeling bad about our mistakes, but rather *owning our humanity*, with gratitude.

The Peace. Like so much in our liturgy, our exchanging a greeting is a basic human action. In our earliest centuries of eucharistic practice, the exchange of a "kiss of peace" (yes, a same-sex kiss on the mouth) was considered the "seal" of our prayers for the Church and the world, perhaps because by ending our prayers with mutual love and friendship, we are giving evidence of the healing of the world, already, right here among us. It might be a Christian

---

8 Ephraim The Syrian (*Homilies* 4:4).

adaptation of the Jewish greeting of peace (*shalom alechem*), as it is still today. It is not necessary to say "peace be with you," although it is natural.

Our greeting each other in the name of Christ is not merely an occasion to catch up with people we have not seen in a week. Nor is it simply an expression of our *natural* loves and friendships, with some in the congregation more than others. Rather, greeting each other at this point is a sign of mutual *reconciliation*. For if God was willing to suffer and die to reconcile with us, how can we possibly not reconcile with each other? And why put it at this point in the service? Well, Jesus said,

> If, therefore, you are bringing your gift to the altar and there recall that your brother holds something against you, leave your gift in front of the altar and first go and be reconciled with your brother; and then come and offer your gift.
>
> Matthew 5:23–24

Three hundred years later John Chrysostom put it rather dramatically: "Let no one who draws near have an enemy! Do you have an enemy? Do not approach! Do you wish to draw near? Be reconciled, and then draw near, and only then touch the Holy Gifts!"[9]

---

9 John Chrysostom, Homily 20.

The Eucharist, Part II:
Eating with God

From the very beginning of our history as follow-ers of Jesus, we have met regularly to eat together. As Andrew McGowan writes, this was ". . . the central act around or within which others—reading and preaching and prophecy—were arranged."[10]

A common feature in the first century Greco-Roman world was the existence of *eating clubs*. Termed *collegia* in Latin or *havurot* in Hebrew, these clubs or societies existed for all manner of purposes: mutual burial insurance, for example, or guilds of artisans associated with a specific profession and its patronal god, or in Jewish practice, associations of rabbis and their disciples. They met from time to time for a banquet in honor of their patron.

The pattern of the event had been set by the Greeks: first they ate together, then the host offered a long toast praising the god and the second part of the evening, the *symposium* or drinking party, began. The earliest eucharists probably followed the same pattern, the sharing of stories, scriptures and songs coming *after* everyone had eaten, just as pagans would have had philosophical or political conversations during the symposium. A few gener-

10 Andrew McGowan, *Ancient Christian Worship: Early Church Practices in Social, Historical and Theological Perspective* (Grand Rapids, MI: Baker Academic, 2014), 20ff and *passim*.

ations later, however, the eucharist had developed the basic structure we have to this day: talk first, then eat.

The procession of gifts. Meals require food, and so the second part of our eucharist begins with the procession of the gifts. In the East, the bread and wine were brought out of the sacristy by deacons and placed on the Holy Table or altar. In the West, however, the people themselves brought all manner of offerings (even cheese, olives, and so forth, on special occasions) to the Holy Table where they were received by the deacons. They chose a loaf and some wine for the eucharist and the rest was set aside to be distributed among the poor.

Today, some parishes have recovered the practice and a full procession of the people bringing gifts takes place from time to time. As significant action, this procession of the gifts is a ritualization not only of our gratitude to God, but of our stewardship: our responsibility to keep the church budget in the black, yes, but more importantly to support our work of healing and transforming the world, beginning with the neediest in the local community. Our gratitude to God is expressed in love of neighbor. This includes setting aside, as the canons of the Church establish, at least one collection a month for the needs of the local poor. The deacon or priest receives the gifts directly from the people at the Holy Table, selecting bread and wine for our offering, and setting the table.

We give thanks. By the end of the first century the long toast in honor of our patron God, Christ, had been transformed into a prayer of praise for the work of God in Jesus. One such prayer has come down to us in the *Didache*, a church manual dating from the time. It assumes that thanks were given over wine and bread at the beginning of the meal, which concluded with the following longer prayer of thanks and praise over a cup of wine:

> ... But after you are satisfied, give thanks thus: We give thanks to you, O Holy Father, for your holy name which you caused to dwell in our hearts, and for the knowledge, and faith and immortality to us through Jesus your child. To you be glory unto the ages. You Lord Almighty made all things for your name's sake, and gave food and drink to humans for their enjoyment, that they might give thanks to you, but to us you have given spiritual food and drink and the life of the Age through your child. Above all we give thanks to you because you are powerful. To you be glory unto the ages. Let grace come and this world go away. Hosanna to the God of David. If someone is holy,

let them come. If they are not, let them
change their hearts. *Maranatha.* Amen.[11]

The Didache's Eucharistic Prayer or Great Thanksgiving shows several important meanings very early on. First, it understands Christ as God's child (or
servant—it is the same word), and a descendant of
King David, therefore with a messianic claim to the
throne. It gives thanks for knowledge, faith, and im-
mortality received through this Davidic King, and
describes the food and drink as "spiritual" in the life
of the Age. What Age? The messianic Age, the Age of
kingdom or Reign of God, already here in our gathering. But why "messianic"? Early eucharists were occasions for getting together to talk and eat in a radically egalitarian context, a sign of God's reign already
here among us. Around the turn of the third century,
Tertullian for example, wrote in North Africa,

> Our feast explains itself by its name. The
> Greeks call it *agape,* i.e., affection. What-
> ever it costs, our outlay in the name of
> piety is gain, since with the good things
> of the feast we benefit the needy;. . . as it
> is with God himself, a peculiar respect

---

11 *Didache*, 10. The concept of "age" (*aeon*) is employed, to indicate
  a very long time—perhaps interminable, since the Reign of God
  would be God's final healing of the world. The members of the
  eucharistic assembly are *already* living in that age. *Maranatha* may
  be translated as either "the Lord has come" or "the Lord is coming."

is shown to the lowly. If the object of our feast be good, in the light of that consider its further regulations. As it is an act of religious service, it permits no vileness or immodesty. The participants, before reclining, taste first of prayer to God. As much is eaten as satisfies the cravings of hunger; as much is drunk as befits the chaste. They say it is enough, as those who remember that even during the night they have to worship God; they talk as those who know that the Lord is one of their auditors. After manual ablution, and the bringing in of lights, each is asked to stand forth and sing, as he can, a hymn to God, either one from the holy Scriptures or one of his own composing,—a proof of the measure of our drinking. As the feast commenced with prayer, so with prayer it is closed.[12]

Later, by the time of Justin, the one presiding began the Great Thanksgiving, or Eucharistic Prayer over the bread and wine. As Justin noted, the one presiding,

> . . . gives glory to the Father of the universe, through the name of the Son and

---

12 Tertullian, *Apology*, 39: 16–18.

of the Holy Spirit, and offers thanks at considerable length for our being counted worthy to receive these things at His hands. And when he has concluded the prayers and thanksgivings, all the people present express their assent by saying *Amen*. This word *Amen* answers in the Hebrew language to *genoito* [so be it]. And when the president has given thanks, and all the people have expressed their assent, those who are called by us deacons give to each of those present to partake of the bread and wine mixed with water over which the thanksgiving was pronounced, and to those who are absent they carry away a portion.[13]

In Justin's time, the Great Thanksgiving may have been improvised but by the mid-fourth century, it had developed much the structure it has today.

The one who presides first greets us with "The Lord be with you."[14] Engaging us in a dialogue she

---

13 Justin Martyr, *Apologia* I, 65.

14 The phrase in Hebrew is *Adonai immachem* (the Lord with you). In Greek it is *ho theos sou* (the Lord with you). In Latin, *dominus vobiscum* (the Lord with you). It is the greeting of the angel to Mary in Luke, and might be better understood not as, "*May* the Lord be with you," but as "The Lord *is* with you,"—perhaps a phrase in common usage at the time. It may well be the Christian equivalent of the Sanskrit *namaste*.

adds, "Lift up your hearts," and "Let us give thanks to the Lord our God," and we agree. The prayer begins; it consists of several sections or moments. The first, the Preface or introduction to the whole prayer, expresses thanks and praise to God for creation and redemption—sometimes with the insertion of some words appropriate to a particular occasion. Then we sing a hymn of praise, the *Sanctus*, and the rest of the Great Thanksgiving continues.

After recalling Christ's coming, we give the warrant for what we are doing: "On the night he was betrayed, he took bread. . . and the cup of wine. . . do this in memory of me. . . ." indicating that these were his body and blood about to be broken and shed for the forgiveness of sins, and that we should repeat the action in his memory.

And so we do. We *remember* not only his last supper with his disciples, but his death, resurrection, and ascension. We *offer* our "sacrifice" of thanks and praise, "presenting from your creation this bread and this wine." We then *invoke* the Holy Spirit upon the gifts and upon us, "that they may be for us the Body of your Son and his Blood of the new covenant. . ." asking to be united to him in his self-offering. We finish with praise to the Father, Son and Holy Spirit, and our Amen.

Note the *we*. The Great Thanksgiving is proclaimed in the plural, not because the bishop or priest is the queen of England, but because it is *our* prayer, the

whole Church's prayer, voiced by the priest but inef-
fective without our consent.

Additionally the Great Thanksgiving is addressed
to the Father, through the Son, in the Holy Spirit. The
whole Trinity is involved in it as we recall and thank
God for creation and the history of God's saving, healing deeds, coming to a head "in these the last days"
with the incarnation, life, ministry, death, resurrection, and ascension of Christ, and the sending of the
Spirit upon the Church. It culminates with our Amen.

Over the centuries, theologians have agonized
over the question whether there is a moment of consecration. The bread, which was mere bread, is, by
the time the prayer ends, Body of Christ, and the
same with the wine, become Blood. The West decided that the moment was in the words "this is
my body" and "this is my blood." The East places it
at the invocation of the Holy Spirit upon the gifts.
Much earlier, however, before we divided, it was lo-
cated after the whole prayer, the final praise of the
Trinity and our Amen:

> . . . the bread and wine of the eucha-
> rist before the invocation of the holy
> and adorable Trinity were simple bread
> and wine, while after the invocation the
> bread becomes the body of Christ, and
> the wine the blood of Christ.[15]

---

15 Cyril of Jerusalem, *Mystagogical Lecture* I,7.

So it is reasonable to surmise that by the end of the fourth century the transformation of the bread and wine into the Body and Blood was thought to take place throughout and by the end of the prayer. The need to spot a "moment of consecration" had not yet surfaced.

We share the meal. Today our meal is simple, and we still break the bread in order to share it. Increasingly congregations use real bread as the first Christians did, a single loaf to be broken into smaller pieces, large enough to chew. Their eucharists were simple meals: mostly bread with vegetables, the occasional fish. They probably avoided fowl and meat, since these to be butchered, had to be sacrificed to idols first.

Did participants eat and drink bread and wine separately, with special devotion (the *Didache* indicates so, as they are an element of Jewish grace at meals), or did they share this bread and wine throughout the whole meal? In any case, the meal eventually dropped out, probably due to increasing numbers, leaving only bread and wine by the late third century. But what does our sharing the Supper of the Lord mean? What has it meant to most of us in its long history? Let us look at the different facets of this meaning.

Eating in memory of Jesus. As Americans, we do not often eat in memory of someone, except perhaps after funerals. Mexicans remember and eat with the dead, on the Day of the Dead, November 2. A meal is prepared with the deceased's favorite foods and then shared at the grave or at home. This practice actually goes back to the very first centuries: Christians, like most Romans, would gather in catacombs to share a meal at the grave of their loved ones, usually on the anniversary of their death. So, it may have seemed completely natural to have a meal in memory of Jesus. This memorial meal, for Roman Christians in the catacombs and other Christians across the area, quickly became enriched with diverse layers of meaning.

Eating in the Reign of God. Isaiah had looked forward to a time when Israel and the nations would be gathered by God in a messianic banquet:

> On this mountain the Lord of hosts will make for all peoples a feast of fat things, a feast of wine on the lees, of fat things full of marrow, of wine on the lees well refined. And he will destroy on this mountain the covering that is cast over all peoples, the veil that is spread over all nations. He will swallow up death forever, and the Lord God will wipe away tears from all faces, and the reproach of his people he will take away from all the earth, for the Lord has spo-

ken. It will be said on that day, "Lo, this
is our God; we have waited for him, that
he might save us."

Isaiah 25:6–9

From the beginning of our history, we understood
our shared meal to be a sign—evidence, if you will—
of the Reign of God arriving already here, among us,
in our fledgling community: the Community of the
Reign of God, an alternative society where ". . . the
blind see again, the lame walk, lepers are cleansed
and the destitute are given good tidings and the poor
hear the good news" (Matthew 11:5). As sacraments
do, this shared meal both expressed and *effected* this
vision of who we are as a community.

Eating in solidarity with the poor. The first eucharists,
likely to have started in Galilee, took place during a
time in which the increasing Roman taxation necessary to build the new cities of Sepphoris and Tibe-
rias caused the expropriation of lands whose owners
could not pay their debts. This increased the ranks
of the landless, but also of the destitute. It is in this
context that the earliest Christians began to have
their shared potlucks, where the poor and hungry
would eat side by side with the more comfortable
and the very, very few wealthy. This connection between the eucharist and the poor was later voiced by
John Chrysostom:

Do you wish to honor the body of the
Saviour? Do not despise it when it is naked. Do not honor it in church with silk
vestments while outside you are leaving
it numb with cold and naked. He who
said, "This is my body," and made it so
by his word, is the same that said, "You
saw me hungry and you gave me no food.
As you did it not to one of the least of
these, you did it not to me." Honor him
then by sharing your property with the
poor. For what God needs is not golden
chalices but golden souls.[16]

Today we continue to rediscover the connection. At
St. Gregory Nyssen Church, in San Francisco, California, for example, immediately following the eucharist each Sunday, the sanctuary becomes a food
distribution center for those who need it. Perhaps
we can once again recover a eucharist where the
comfortable and the destitute eat side by side?

We, the Body of Christ. Reading the earliest account
we have of Christians eating together at eucharists
(1 Corinthians), one is struck by Paul's rhetorical
move: in order to demand that the rich respect the
poor and stop eating separately the delicacies they
brought, he argues that Christians are nothing less

16 John Chrysostom, *Homilies on Matthew*, 50, 3.

than the Body of the risen Christ. To prove it, he repeats Jesus's words about the bread and wine while saying the Jewish grace at the Last Supper. Thus, for Paul the meaning of our eating together is the same as his conversion experience on the road to Damascus: Christians are Christ, and by persecuting them, he was persecuting Christ. Much later Augustine would sum it up nicely: "Behold who you are, become what you receive."[17] And John Chrysostom would explain,

> This union is effected through the food that he has given us in his desire to show the love he has for us. For this reason he united himself intimately with us, he blended his body with ours like leaven, so that we should become one single entity, as the body is joined to the head.[18]

Eating Christ. Gradually, the mystical experience of individually eating Christ and being united to him took hold among those few who regularly received communion during the Middle Ages. Hadewijch of Antwerp, for example, wrote of the experience in the thirteenth century:

---

17 Augustine, Easter Sermon, 227.
18 John Chrysostom, *Homilies on John*, 46, 3.

> At that time I also had, for a short while,
> the strength to bear it. But all too soon
> I lost external sight of the shape of that
> beautiful man, [Christ] and I saw him
> disappear to nothing, so quickly melt-
> ing away and fusing together [with me]
> that I could not see or observe him out-
> side of me, nor discern him within me.
> It was to me at that moment as if we
> were one without distinction.[19]

Much ink has been spilled by theologians over twenty centuries trying to explain *how* the bread and wine
are transformed. Apparently the explanation from
the fourth century, that they do so by the praying of
the Great Thanksgiving and our final assent, was not
good enough. The earliest explanation understood
the bread and wine as types (signs) of the antitype
(Christ). Much later, the medieval Thomist theory
of transubstantiation—a change in the "substance"
of the bread and wine (what they are), while the "ac-
cidents" (what they look, taste, and smell like) stay
the same—took hold. More recently, "symbolic re-
alism" is more popular with liturgical scholars for
in a sense it joins both the earliest understanding
with the more literal medieval explanation. Think of

---

19 Hadewijch, "Vision VII," *Essential Writings of Christian Mysti-
    cism,* edited by Edward McGuinn (New York: Modern Library,
    2006), 104.

a photo of a loved one, making him present, while not being exactly him. These attempts at explaining *how* are put in their place by Queen Elizabeth I's famous ditty:

> *'Twas God the Word that spake it,*
> *He took the Bread and brake it:*
> *And what that Word did make it,*
> *That I believe and take it.*

However we may try to explain how this is possible, Christ is present in our eucharistic action in four different ways at once: In the congregation, his risen Body through baptism; in the proclamation of the Word, for he *is* that Word made flesh; in the Thanksgiving over bread and wine and their consumption; and in the ordained ministers, who as we shall see below, represent Christ because they represent us, Christ's risen Body.

The sending. After eating, we are sent out. In the Book of Common Prayer, this takes place in three "moments": first we ask God to "send us now into the world in peace, and grant us strength and courage to love and serve you with gladness and singleness of heart. . ."[20] then the priest gives an optional blessing and a deacon sends us out.

Our friend the nun Egeria, writing in Jerusalem

---

20 BCP, 365.

in the late fourth century, described how after services the people went "to the bishop's hand." I do not think they went to kiss his ring, but to receive a quick laying on of the hand in a gesture meaning blessing and sending with authority, or commissioning. But commissioning to do what? And where? To proclaim, like Jesus, the Good News of God: the Reign of God is very near; transform your hearts and trust the Good News.

The arc of the eucharist. In sum, the eucharist is composed of the seven signifying actions that we have reviewed; but the whole flow of the event, its arc, if you will, has itself layers of meaning.

First, and throughout the entire liturgy, the eucharist is *God's* action—through our ritual actions, yes, but it is God interacting with us, rehearsing us in how to live in the new world of God's reign. This divine action is dynamic and participatory. It is not a show to be watched or a sport at which we can be spectators, but requires our conscious, active participation. *We all,* and not only the people up at the altar, are doing it together, led by a variety of ministers.

Additionally the arc has a salvific, or if you prefer, healing logic to it: God calls us out of daily life into an assembly in order to heal us and send us back to the world to change and heal it. This "otherness" of the assembly—its being set apart even if temporarily by God—constitutes the eucharist as a holy, or sacred, event, if for no other reason that it helps us to "practice" living with God, consciously and outside of everyday life, and revealing our everyday lives to be sacred as well, full of the presence of God.

Finally, in the eucharist we engage in actions that manifest or disclose our true nature as a community: the continuation, or Body, of Jesus Christ in history so that, as Louis Bouyer wrote, the eucharist is the Epiphany of the Church,[21] the expression of who we are as a people.

The Reign here already and not yet. The eucharist reveals the Church as a community of people called together by God to be transformed and sent into the world to announce the Good News of God's eagerness to reconcile with us unconditionally, restoring and transforming us as a society—and not only as individuals, to the full image of God.

In this way, it presents a *felt experience*—and not only ideas, of this world restored in the Reign of God so that, as in all religious rituals, the participants experience what it is like to live in it as it would be here and now if it were to arrive today. In this sense at least, worship, when it is working well, *is* Christian formation.

Into this community of the Reign, God calls anyone who wishes to join through a process of change dramatically enacted in baptism, in which we join

---

21 Louis Bouyer, *The Church of God: Body of Christ and the Temple of the Spirit* (San Francisco, CA: Ignatius Press, 2011), 322.

Christ in an imitation of his death so as to share in his resurrected life, becoming part of his risen Body. "This mystery is a great one but I am speaking of the Anointed [Christ] and the assembly [Church]," wrote the author of the Letter to the Ephesians (5:32).The resurrection of Christ and the very being of the Church are intimately related.

A note on eucharist without baptism. The current fascination with doing away with baptism as a requirement for participation in the eucharist reveals a desire to be inclusive and radically hospitable to the point of being scandalous. That is certainly a New Testament value and a characteristic of the earliest eucharists, where rich and poor, slave and free, sinners or not, ate together as a sign of the arrival of God's promised reign. On the other hand, the eucharist is the work of God through the sign-actions of Christ's Body, the Church, constituted as a community in baptism. How to settle the matter while honoring both aspects?

At the core of the issue lies a confusion about the nature of norms and exceptions. In sacramental theology, by norm we do not mean "what most people do" (statistical norm) but what the sacrament would be like *in its fullness*, without abbreviations or exceptions. So the norm for baptism is the immersion of the adult candidate within the full congregation on Easter or a major feast day, following a long period of conversion of the heart and behavior and followed in turn by seven weeks of reflection in community on what has taken place. Obviously, we do not do this most of the time. It is the ideal, by which we measure our decisions to make exceptions and adjustments.

In the same way, the norm of the eucharist is the meeting of the Christian assembly for a shared meal, listening to God's word and applying it to our lives, praying for the Church and the world; and offering thanks and praise in memory of Jesus Christ, his life, ministry, death and ongoing life, and the coming of the Spirit, and sending us out into the world to heal it.

The fact that this is a Christian event, however, does not mean that we have to become liturgical policemen at the communion rail. All norms admit exceptions, and certainly we must make exceptions in the name of love and radical hospitality, welcoming all to the Table without questioning their ecclesiastical membership, while making sure that we preach and teach about baptism.

That does *not* mean, however, that the one presiding should add words of invitation to the existing invitation, "the Gifts of God for the People of God," making an issue out of a confusion. Such invitations, if at all needed, are best added at the end of the sermon, or printed in the bulletin. For it is one thing to make pastoral exceptions to the canon that requires baptism before eucharist. We do it all the time. It is a whole other thing to stop the liturgy and proclaim (as if one had authority to do so), that baptism is not how we become members of Christ's risen Body, the Church. That is a serious error in liturgical theology, and although all norms admit exceptions, to make exceptions into norms has been one of the most dangerous and long-lasting mistakes in the history of worship through twenty centuries.

So far we have taken a close look at baptism, which make us members of Christ and his community of the Reign of God, the Church; and we also explored the Holy Eucharist, which week by week celebrates the mystery of Christ and His Church, the Community of the Reign of God. We turn now to look at how our community is organized.

Chapter V

Getting Organized

Holy Order

For much of Christian history, certainly for the almost thousand years that the Middle Ages lasted, too often "Church" meant "clergy." We have, however, recovered to a greater or lesser extent the ancient understanding of the Church as the community of those baptized into the death and resurrection of Jesus, becoming part of his risen Body. So we might as well ask ourselves: Now that the ordained are not the only "church," what are they?

Begin with your experience. What has been your experience of ministry? First, of your own ministry, but also of your bishop's, priest's, and deacon's ministries? What characteristics does all ministry, by anyone, have in common? How are the ministries of the four orders of the Church—laity, bishops, deacons, and priests—different from each other? What has your experience of ordained ministers been like? Exciting? Meaningful? Troubling? Consoling? Illuminating? Think for a minute of how ordained ministers have or have not played a part in your past. Think also of your expectations of clergy—how they have or have not been fulfilled. You may want to take notes.

What is ministry? The word means *service*. All Christians are called to service *by virtue of our baptism.* This service is not mainly service to the rest of the Church (by serving on the altar guild, or being an usher or acolyte, for example), but to the world. So we must ask ourselves, in what ways is the service of ordained ministers *different* from the service of the baptized though not ordained?

The orders of the Church. Some people may assume that by Holy Orders we mean that the bishop (or God) has commanded the clergy to do something, as in, "I order you to. . . ," but the term actually comes from *ordo*, the Latin word for arrangement, classification, or structure. Like any human community, the Christian People have an order. Since we are a "chosen kindred, a royal priesthood, a holy nation," (1 Peter 2:9) that order is holy.

The term laity, employed to denote those baptized but not ordained, is derived from *laos*, the people, for we are the *laos theou,* the "People of God." Israel was the first "People of God," but the Church, as a development out of ancient Israel, has claimed the title as well. Isn't *everyone* "people of God" you may well ask. Yes, in the sense that every human being is a creature of and belongs to God. The expression "People of God," however, also means, a people *chosen* by God for a purpose. In the New Testament, the Church is an assembly, or *ekklesia*, called out and chosen by God from the rest of the world—and therefore set apart or consecrated, and so "the People of God." In a sense, the term implies that Jews and Christians consciously claim and are revealed as what everyone else is: a child of God with a purpose. Our purpose, or mission, like Christ's, is reconciliation: with each other and with God, healing the world, welcoming God's Reign in the process. In the final chapter, we will explore the People of God, the Church, as a sign and sacrament gathered by God and sent out in mission. Here, however, we take a look at bishops, deacons, and priests, that is, to the *ordained*.

Ordination. Perhaps the most shocking thing about an ordination service is that the people tell the bishop what to do: "*N.*, Bishop in the Church of God, on behalf of the clergy and people of the Diocese of *N.*, we present to you *N.N.* to be ordained a priest in Christ's holy catholic Church."[1] The second is that the candidate shows up dressed in her baptismal garment, the alb, the dress of the laity, and not the distinctive dress of any other order to which she may already belong. These two small details are meant to convey two important aspects of ordination. First, *it is the Church community* that initiates the ordination by asking the bishop to ordain. Second, *the one to be ordained is a baptized member of the Church,* and is ordained on that basis, *not on his already having been*

---

1 BCP, 526. Ordination of bishops (BCP, 513) and deacons (BCP, 538) is similar.

in another order. It *is* a requirement of canon law for priests to have been deacons and bishops to have been priests, but that requirement is not present in the rite.

The bishop, after confirming that the candidate has been properly selected and prepared, solemnly asks the congregation if it is their will that the candidate be ordained. We pray for the ordinand, scripture readings follow, and a sermon. The bishop examines the candidate, describing the nature of the order to which she is called, and she promises to carry out her ministry. The Holy Spirit is invoked in a hymn, and the bishop lays hands on the ordinand asking God to pour grace and power and make her a bishop, priest, or deacon in God's Church. A Bible is handed to the ordinand and possibly additional signs of her ministry, including the appropriate liturgical garments. The new bishop, priest, or deacon is presented to the people, who cheer, and the Peace is shared. The newly ordained participates in the rest of the eucharist according to their order.

Laying hands. In all three rites of ordination, the laying on of hands by the bishop with prayer is the core of the rite. Laying on of hands with prayer was already a Jewish way to appoint elders and rabbis in Israel, and the first apostles did just that to appoint Matthias and the first seven deacons. The gesture expressed selection, authorization, and commissioning to go and do something.

Leadership in the early Church. The earliest forms of Church leadership—itinerant prophets and preachers and house-church hosts—eventually gave place to a threefold expression of the ministry of leadership in community that we know today as bishops, deacons, and priests. By the time of the writing of the gospel according to Luke and the book of Acts, in the late first or early second century, there were *episkopoi* (literally "overseers"—our bishops) and *diakonoi* (literally "servants"—our deacons) in liturgical leadership within the Christian assembly. *Presbyteroi* (literally "elders"—our priests) functioned in a different role altogether, not liturgical, but as members of the congregation's council of elders.

Councils of elders in Jewish towns made governing decisions as a kind of city council. Christians, perhaps understanding themselves as a form of alternative village or town, elected them to make decisions regarding the community's common life. It is *possible* that these Christian councils of elders, besides exercising general oversight of the local community, also gathered the community, preached, taught the faith, and ministered to the sick. But *presbyteroi*, or priests, were first of all members of a *governing body*—more like our vestries than persons presiding in the liturgy. Presiding was done by the *episkopos* (bishop), assisted by *diakonoi* (deacons).

By the third quarter of the first century, for example, the *Didache* instructs Christians,

> Appoint therefore for yourselves over-
> seers (*episkopoi*) and servants (*dia-
> konoi*) worthy of the Lord, humble men,
> and not lovers of money, and truthful
> and approved, for they also minister
> to you the ministry of the prophets
> and teachers. Therefore do not despise
> them, for they are your honourable
> men together with the prophets and
> teachers.[2]

We already see local communities appointing bishops and deacons besides prophets and teachers. The
presbyters are there, too, but as a *governing* council.

Initially each congregation had a bishop as its
head, and since there was a congregation in each
town, bishops were easily associated with it. Gradually, though, the various congregations (and their
bishops) in a large city like Rome or Antioch were
brought under the authority of a single bishop. This
unity of the Christian community under a single
bishop in a city with many congregations became a
bone of contention, but eventually the single bishop
over all the congregations in a city became the norm.

Delegation of liturgical presidency. One Sunday morning, probably after the turn of the third century, a
bishop in a large city turned to his wife and likely

---

2 *Didache*, ch. 15.

said, "Honey, I can't be in twenty congregations in one day!" Or perhaps the persecutions in the mid-third century reduced the availability of bishops and sent congregations into hiding. Either way, bishops began to delegate presidency at the eucharist to a local presbyter of the governing council in a given congregation. To make it crystal clear that this was a delegation and that the real president of the assembly remained the bishop, he would send a piece of the consecrated bread from an earlier eucharist to the local community. There, the appointed presbyter would drop it in the chalice. This was called the *fermentum* (leaven)—an indication of the delegation of presidency to the presbyter by the bishop.

"Priest" (*presbyteros*) and "priest" (*hiereus*). Christian literature after the third century sometimes calls the bishop a "high priest." This can be confusing as the reference is to the former chief priest (*hiereus*) in Jerusalem, *not to the presbyters of Christian congregations*. During the first three centuries, Christians called no one priest (*hiereus*) in the same way the word was used in the temple; only Christ, who as both sacrificer and victim on the cross ended the practice of ritual sacrifice, received that term. Early Christians did recognize themselves as a "royal priesthood," though, in a metaphorical sense, offering themselves to God in daily life and interceding for the world. Only in the fourth century did the term for temple priest (*hiereus*) come to be associated with the bishops, and much later, with the presbyters (*presbyteroi*).

By the time of the Council of Nicea (325 CE) our threefold structure of ordained ministry was in place. Besides bishops, deacons, and priests, however, we also had other orders: catechumens preparing for baptism, widows, virgins, and penitents. Later on, in the Middle Ages, there would also be exorcists, bell ringers, lectors, porters, and so forth—a plethora of "minor orders" possibly originating in monasteries, which by the eighth century had begun to strongly influence the development of worship. The Protestant Reformers did away with most orders—certainly with the minor orders. In our day, while nomenclature and theology may vary, the three categories remain the same, even if understood differently, in many denominations.

Order as relationship. At the most basic level, to be ordained is to be put in one's place within the Church structure, in relation to both the Church and the rest of the world. These positions developed naturally, expressing in worship the same type of leadership that people had in the everyday life of the community and its surroundings. I am often asked, immediately after finding out that I am a priest, "Do you have a church?" It is as if being a priest went hand in hand with serving a congregation. There is wisdom in this, for without the people, there is neither "priest nor steeple." The ordained—even bishops—

are so within and because of the Christian community, and not above, besides, or regardless of it.

The ordained are also specific *icons* of different aspects of the whole Christian community, for in ordination a regular human being is made into a *sign*. People as signs are quite common, really; we run into them all the time. They might be signs of a system of justice (police, judges, and so forth), or are signs of a system of health (nurses, doctors, technicians), or of military power. Clergy are signs of the Church, the Body of Christ, and therefore of Christ, God's incarnation. For the whole Christian community, *is* apostolic, servant, and a welcoming and forming host to the rest of the world. The ordained are the signs of these gifts of the Spirit conferred on the whole Church. And so each order manifests or exemplifies a different aspect of the Church.

The bishop as sign. Bishops, as *episkopoi* (overseers) have the far and wide view of things. Additionally, they express three aspects of the Church: Its unity, apostolicity, and catholicity. By being an individual, and not a committee, the bishop embodies the unity of the Church. This unity is not an unfulfilled hope, but a fundamental aspect of who we already are. We believe in one Church, we say in the Creed, not that there *will be* one Church but that it is *already* one. One Body of Christ, one with Christ through baptism, and one Christ who is one with the Father. The Church *is* one. The single person of the bishop is a sign of it. Our rifts and separations are contrary to our true nature: to be one community, one Body.

The bishop is also the living icon of the Church's *apostolicity*. We are an apostolic community because we are sent (*apostolein* means "to send with authority") like the apostles, and because we are in continuity with the apostles' teaching and community, the breaking of the bread, and the prayers. By ordaining others, bishops also express the Church's authority to set up its leadership.

The bishop also expresses the catholicity or universality of the Church, precisely because being the *episcopos*, or overseer, she has the longer, wider view of things—not only of the whole diocese, but of the rest of the Christian communities represented by their bishops locally and around the world. In this way, the bishop helps prevent us from becoming too provincial and local, and reminds us that we belong to a universal, that is, catholic, Church.

The ministry of bishop requires a whole raft of virtues, not least humility enough to care for oneself. Another one is authority, which often gets confused with power. But authority (the ability to engender trust in your judgment, because you can *author*, that is, get the job done) is granted gradually as trustworthiness is established. On the other hand, power is the right to command, invested by office, job description, or canons. Power is *canonical*. Authority is *relational*. This is true not only of bishops, of course, but of priests and deacons as well.

The priest as sign. A presbyter or priest (from Old French, *preste*—a contraction of *presbytère*, from the Greek *presbyteros,* that is, elder, or old person) expresses the *eldership* of the Church and receives by delegation some aspects of the bishop's own liturgical presidency. This delegation, implicit in ordination, includes the delegation of presiding not only in the liturgical life of the congregation, but in its common life, as well. Aspects of a priest's presidency outside the liturgy include welcoming, pastoring, teaching, and leading a local Christian congregation, just as the whole Church is called to welcome, pastor, teach, and lead. In congregations without deacons, their ministries, both liturgical and extra-liturgical, fall to the priest as presider, with the assistance of lay leaders.

The development of the priesthood, however, often degraded into what Louis Weil has termed "the omnivorous priest."[3] By that, he means a priest who in the liturgy (and even in everyday life) often does *everything*. Some priests brag that they have to change the light bulbs. I would not, as that is a clear sign that delegation is absent, and one cannot preside well without delegating. Additionally, presiding literally means sitting in front. Sitting. Not running around doing everything.

---

3 Often repeated personal communication.

Take, for example the Holy Eucharist, Rite II in
the Book of Common Prayer: If there is another
preacher and a deacon, the one presiding has very
little to say—a greeting, two collects, the absolution,
the Eucharistic Prayer, and the optional final blessing. *Nothing more.* This allows her to truly preside
as an attentive, calm, non-anxious presence in the
liturgy, modeling a community that gathers to listen
to the Word, shares its meaning, prays for Church
and world, and eats together in order to be sent out.
A priest *leads* all this implicitly, through delegation
and the wise and effective support of multiple liturgical ministers: lectors, ushers, music director and
singers, the altar guild, acolytes, and so forth.

The deacon as sign. Early on, to be a *diakonos* (literally
"one who walks through the dust," that is, a servant),
or deacon, meant that one had been delegated by the
bishop to assist in worship, administer the congregation, and coordinate the distribution of assistance
to the poor. Deacons developed because the apostles
had to preach and were not always able to serve tables. Rather quickly, they also became community
organizers. After all, serving a meal to fifty to a hundred people requires just that: organizational skill.
What did they organize? The Church in its ministry
to the world. Today deacons can and perhaps should
organize the congregation's ministry outreach to the
surrounding world. They cannot possibly do it all
themselves, but, again, by delegation, can keep sev-

eral, even many local ministries going, encouraging and organizing volunteers, managing budgets, and so forth. Thus, though the word means servant, deacons are not *mere* servants (all the baptized are supposed to be servants), but the leaders of a servant church. They are to bring the needs of the world to the attention of the Church—and organize us to do something about it.

Icons of Christ. As signs of different aspects of the Church, the ordained ministers re-present the Church and therefore Christ. We do not represent Christ because we have a direct metaphysical connection to him or are especially saintly, but because we are *signs or icons of his Church, his Body*. The baptized do too, of course, insofar as they are known to be Christian, but the ordained are *officially* set up as signs.

Ontological change. Too often, this unusual phrase is used to describe the holiness or sacrality of the ordained as an inscrutable, mystical thing that takes place in ordination and lasts forever. To understand its meaning we have to step back to the meaning of ontology, a branch of philosophy that asks *what beings are*. Is it a plane? A train? Superman? Is it an elephant or an insect? What sort of being is, for example, a unicorn?—a horse with a horn, imaginary. What matters to ontology is what a being *is*. *An ontological change is a change in what one is.*

So what sort of being was Mother Jennifer before she was ordained? Jennifer was a woman. Once ordained, however, she becomes *a woman who is a sign.* A change has taken place. Without ceasing to be a woman, Jennifer is now a woman-sign. This is a real change—and of course it stems from and effects a change in her relationships, within the Church and beyond it.

In sum, the orders of the Church are expressions of different aspects of the whole Church, They arise out of our need to organize ourselves as a community and exist *within, for, and because of* that community, and its witness in service to the world. They do not exist apart from the Church and its common life.

Chapter VI

Sign of God's Love

Marriage

Of all the rites of the Church, marriage is the most recent and varied. As we have it now, it is probably no more than five hundred years old. Before we examine it, however, let us look at what marriage means to you, in your experience.

Your experience. What is it like for you to attend a wedding? Think of your memories, stories, and meaningful moments, but also puzzlements, annoyances, and bewilderments. What was it like to get married, if you were? How would you characterize the difference between a church wedding and a civil marriage? Think also about the *relationship* between two people that is marriage: What aspects of your relationship with your spouse do you find most important? If you are single, what aspects do you find are most important in married couples' relationships? In your experience, what roles do family members, friends, neighbors, and coworkers play in the health of a marriage?

Since our quest is for the layered meanings of worship, we will reduce this chapter to a discussion of the *rite* of marriage in the Book of Common

Prayer and its analogues initially developed to include couples of the same sex, but now available to all. We are not going to be referring to civil marriage in and of itself.

The marriage rite. In a marriage service we gather to witness and bless the joining together of a couple in Holy Matrimony. The officiant explains the nature, purpose, and theology of marriage. The couple is a sign of the love of Christ and his Church. Their union is for mutual joy, help, and comfort in prosperity and adversity; and, if God wills, for the procreation of children.[1] If there are no objections, we proceed to the Declaration of Consent, and the congregation agrees to support the couple in their marriage. The Declaration of Consent was originally *the rite of betrothal* or engagement, held months, or even years, before the marriage. It slowly crept into the marriage rite proper, as we have it today. The officiant then prays God to assist the couple to live out their vows. Readings chosen from a variety of possibilities follow, and the sermon.

Then the marriage, properly speaking, takes place. The couple pronounce their vows, and the officiant may ask God's blessing on a ring(s) as a sign of the vows binding the couple together. We pray for the couple and those present, asking, among other things, for wisdom and devotion in their life; mutual

---

1   BCP, 423 ff.

forgiveness when they hurt each other; and that they may be a sign of Christ's love for the world. They are not married only for each other and their offspring. We also ask that they may reach out in love and concern for others, that all married persons present may find their lives strengthened and their loyalties confirmed.

The officiant then blesses and thanks God and asks for God's blessing upon the marriage. We give thanks for God's tender love in sending Jesus Christ, consecrating marriage in his name, and invoke God's blessing upon the couple, that their love be "a seal upon their hearts, a mantle about their shoulders, and a crown upon their foreheads." A blessing in the name of the Trinity follows and the couple is pronounced married, with an admonition not to tear them asunder. If the eucharist is not to follow, the service concludes with the Lord's Prayer, and the Peace. If the eucharist follows, the service continues with the Peace.

A brief history of the rite. It took the Church a long time to come to this type of marriage service, perhaps because Christians originally understood marriage to be a civil affair, a legal contract binding the couple together. Gradually, however, we began to bless the bride, then the couple, and kept adding elements for a variety of reasons.

For early Christians the ideal human state was celibacy, not marriage, which was considered a concession to the needs of the flesh and our humanity. To choose the single life, without sexual relationships, was, to say the least, a radical choice to make, and a sign of expecting the imminent return of Christ. As centuries passed, celibacy was further elevated out of an increasingly ascetical emphasis and suspicion of the body.

By the fourth century the bride began to receive a blessing at the home—a prayer asking God for her fertility. There is also some evidence of religious weddings from the sixth century onward; the Verona Sacramentary for example includes a prayer for the veiling of a bride.

Marriage was not considered a sacrament until 1184. Even so, in the West the couple were (and still are) considered the ministers of the marriage; the Church only witnesses and blesses it. Through the Middle Ages, marriages generally took place between the two persons by simply saying "I marry you" (not "I will marry you," which legally constituted betrothal, or engagement). With few exceptions, usually among the nobility, European marriages took place by mutual consent and a declaration of marriage and its sexual consummation. Vows and declaration of marriage were not added to the rite until the late Middle Ages. The Protestant reformers did not consider marriage a sacrament and their rites, for the first time, declared its purpose to be for mutual joy and support, and not always for the generation of children.

Early same-sex marriage. In 1994 John Boswell published *Same Sex Unions in Premodern Europe*, claiming that several early medieval codices from Eastern Europe contained a rite for same-sex unions very similar to marriage.[2] These, dubbed "the making of brothers," (*adelphopoiesis*) do not actually say that the two persons are being *married*, and critics therefore condemned the author for being tendentious. The rites themselves however, are clearly modeled on marriage, especially their ceremonial (joining hands over the gospel book, crowning, and walking together around the altar). Sometimes actions speak louder than words.

The couple as sign. Like all rites, the marriage rite is composed of signs, and of these, the most fundamental in marriage is the couple *themselves*, for their love for each other is a sign of God's presence between them, and of the love of Christ for his Church, as well as God's love and faithfulness toward all creation. Other signs, like the vows, joining hands, and the blessing over the couple assume and express the nature of the couple's relationship in love. Equally important is the Christian community's honoring of the relationship, our celebration and gratitude for it, and our support of the couple.

---

2 John Boswell, *Same-Sex Unions in Pre-Modern Europe* (New York: Random House, 1994).

Commitment and blessing. The former bishop of Portsmouth, Kenneth Stevenson, wrote two books on the history and theology of marriage. In them, he makes the case that the essential aspects of a marriage rite are *commitment* and *blessing*. By commitment, he did not mean, necessarily, vows, as these came into the rite in the late Middle Ages, but commitment to a life together characterized by faithfulness, fidelity, ability to trust and be trustworthy, and so forth. Too often, we think of commitment only in terms of sexual exclusivity, but there is much more to it than that. In the marriage rite, we acknowledge the couple's commitment as a blessing not only to them and us, but to all others as well. We thank and praise God, asking God in turn to bless the couple.

Jewish blessings always bless God first, and then ask that God grant a blessing in return. This structure survives in the Roman nuptial prayer found in the sixth century Verona Sacramentary and in our marriage rite; it is typical also of our Eucharistic Prayers, the blessing of baptismal water, and the Easter proclamation at the Easter Vigil: we praise and bless God first and then ask for a blessing on the bread and wine, the water, or the Easter candle. Similarly, in marriage we first thank and praise God, and then ask God's blessing on the couple. In more recent centuries, however, we have abridged the blessing, keeping only its second part, asking God to bless, or declaring that God does, with the unfortunate result our thanks and praise are left out, and "receiving the blessing of the church" sounds like receiving approval or sanction. The Church's blessing of the couple is better understood not as a sanction or approval but thanksgiving to God for the couple, their love, and what these represent.

Sign of God's love, not gender. The Jewish and Christian traditions see in the couple a sign of the relationship, either between Yahweh and Israel, or Christ and his Church. In the case of heterosexual marriages, however, it is easy to fall into the trap of thinking that God and Christ must be male and Israel or the Church female. The comparison, though, is not about gender, nor about who is superior to whom, but about God's *faithfulness*. The same image applies in the case of same-sex couples. A couple's commitment to each other in love is a sign of God's commitment to us and our response, regardless of gender, is thanks and praise.

Sign of God's reign. In the Eastern Churches, the couple is crowned during the rite, indicating that they are royalty: they are the authority in their household, and their love represents to us a sign of God's reign. This detail appears also in our blessing over the couple where we pray that their love be ". . . a seal upon their hearts, a mantle about their shoulders, and a crown upon their foreheads."[3] The allusion to

---

3 BCP, 430

a mantle comes from the Old Spanish ("Mozarabic") rite of marriage and survives to this day in the Latino custom of wrapping the couple in a mantle or tying a cord around them, along with the transfer of *arras*—coins—between the two.

Modern same-sex marriage. You may have noticed that I have striven to describe marriage and its meanings regardless of the gender of the couple. That's because the Episcopal Church celebrates same-sex marriages, and its marriage rite has been adapted now to include same-sex couples, and another rite developed also reveals the same theology. There is no theological difference between heterosexual and homosexual marriage in the Episcopal Church. Rather, both are understood to be rites involving blessing God for a committed relationship and asking God's blessing upon the couple and beyond.

Thus Christian marriage and its celebration as a wedding is founded on the commitment of the couple in love, celebrated by the Christian assembly as a sign of God's faithful love to all of creation, a blessing upon each other, their family and friends, and the wider community. It is also a sign of God's promised Reign of truth, justice, peace, and love here on earth.

Chapter VII

In a New Place

Anointing of the Sick

I n the rite of the Anointing of the Sick, we anoint a person with oil, praying for healing and peace.

Your experience. How have you experienced anointing, either of yourself or others? What aspects of that rite did you find moving, engaging, puzzling, questionable, exciting or boring? What do you remember? What would we have lost if the rite did not exist?

The rite. Many congregations celebrate the eucharist in the middle of the week, with anointing of the sick. Generally before the Peace, the priest anoints the forehead of those who present themselves with oil blessed by the priest or bishop and with the words, "N., I lay my hands upon you in the Name of the Father, and of the Son, and of the Holy Spirit, beseeching our Lord Jesus Christ to sustain you with his presence, to drive away all sickness of body and spirit, and to give you that victory of life and peace which will enable you to serve him both now and evermore. Amen."[1]

---

1   BCP, 456.

This, however, is an abbreviation of the rite contained in the prayer book, which indicates that the words above should be accompanied by the laying on of hands. Anointing with oil is optional. Thus the rite actually involves either laying on of hands, or laying on of hands with anointing.

Biblical anointing. In the ancient Near East anointing a person with oil was a mark of a change in *status or condition*, such as at betrothals, or when deputizing a delegate. Israel borrowed the custom, but used it ritually to mark the raising up of kings, priests, and prophets. The word "Messiah," for example, comes from the Hebrew *messiach*, meaning anointed, that is, *chosen*. In Greek the same word is *Christos*. This is why Jesus is sometimes called "the Anointed One."

The anointing of kings, priests, and prophets, as in our rite with the sick, was a sign of being inwardly anointed by the Spirit of God. This reinforced the idea of being chosen and given divine authority to exercise one's office. In baptism we, too, were anointed as a sign of our being reborn into a "holy nation, a royal priesthood." Today, in the case of anointing of the sick, the act also carries the meaning of being anointed with God's grace and Spirit.

Anointing for healing and more. The Old Testament also requires anointing for the rehabilitation of certain ill persons and we still anoint the sick, following the exhortation in the Letter of James,

Is anyone among you ill? Let him sum-
mon the elders of the assembly, and let
them pray over him, having anointed
him with oil in the name of the Lord.
And the prayer of faith will save the one
who is ailing, and the Lord will raise
him up, and if he should be someone
who has committed sins it will be forgiven him.

James 5:14–15

Our anointing the sick, however, is more than a
prayer for healing. Since anointing expresses a recognition of a change in status, it also recognizes a
shift in the ill person's *relationship to himself and to
the community.* Particularly in our culture of "self-
made" men and women, we are too easily tempted
to deny our need for help from others. Anointing,
especially when it is done in the full assembly of
Christians on a Sunday, can be very powerful, mark-
ing and honoring the person's new relationship to
those around them, for example, at a major stage of
change, such as a serious diagnosis, or when the person must stop working or coming to church.

Take—let us call him Howard—for example. A
faithful member of a parish in San Francisco at the
height of the AIDS crisis in the late 1980s, Howard
succumbed gradually to the disease. Occasionally he
would come to a healing service with anointing on

Wednesdays. One Sunday, however, he showed up with two pillows, for he was so sick that he wanted to lay down in a pew through the whole service. It was clear that Howard would soon cease coming to church entirely. After the service, I asked if he would like us to anoint him the following Sunday. He did, and so we did, as he stood in the middle aisle, the congregation laying hands upon him as I poured oil on his head. Not only were we praying God for healing for Howard, we as a community were acknowledging a major step in his illness, expressing our support physically in a rite, and recognizing him as being now in a new relationship to us.

Anointing as ordination into the Order of the Sick. Precisely because anointing may mark a change in relationships, it resembles ordination, which we discussed previously. In this case, the order (meaning place or category) into which the sick person is welcomed is the order of the sick. Like the ordained, the sick person is recognized as a living *icon* of something. In anointing, the ill person is "placed" in a new perspective as a *living image of the suffering Christ.* Whether we anoint a person often and more casually, or on a major occasion in the person's journey through illness, we call down God's grace upon them and recognize them as icons of Christ.[2]

---

2 James Empereur, *Prophetic Anointing: God's Call to the Sick, the Elderly and the Dying* (Wilmington, DE: Michael Glazier, 1983).

In this light, perhaps we should try to recover one of the central meanings of the eucharist: medicine for the soul. Much of what most people expect and often receive through anointing used to be part of the experience of receiving the eucharist. Have we lost this dimension? Or is the more personal and intimate prayer of the person doing the anointing speaking more clearly to the felt need for physical (and/or spiritual) healing? I wonder. Still, Pope Francis wrote, "The Eucharist, although it is the fullness of sacramental life, is not a prize for the perfect but a powerful medicine and nourishment for the weak."[3]

Either way, anointing and laying hands on a person at a critical time in their lives—a time when their relationships are in the process of changing, and often accompanied by suffering and lack of self-reliance—can signify not only the person's faithful allegiance to God, but God's loving providence as she is assured that the Christian community will also accompany her on the journey ahead.

---

3 *Evangelii Gaudium*, 47.

Chapter VIII

The Uprising of Jesus Christ

The Church, Its Mission, and Culture

Throughout *A House of Meanings,* we have been examining and reflecting on the liturgical life of the Christian Church referring to the rites included in the Book of Common Prayer. We have spent most of our time looking *into* the Church community and its worship. Now it is time for us to stand at the church door and look *out,* taking the wider and farther view, examining the Church as a whole, a Spirited community sent out on a mission.

But first, your experience. What does the Church mean *to you*? Has the meaning been the same over the years? Has it changed and developed? Are the meanings all good? Problematic? What does the Church mean to the people you know at work, in the neighborhood, your friends and acquaintances? You may want to engage some of them in exploring these questions before we start. And, of course, you may want to take notes.

The Church through time. What began twenty centuries ago as a group of followers of Jesus meeting regularly for a meal and announcing the nearness of God's Reign has gone through many changes. As we grew, we were first suspected, later tolerated, then the compulsory religion of the state, soon enough one with the dying Roman Empire, and the *de facto* political power in Europe. As secular states began to appear, we were caught between kings and popes, unsure of which way to turn. Since the Industrial Revolution, we have been considered increasingly irrelevant, first in Europe, and later in the Americas. Over the last few decades, we are often seen as suspect of being either stupid, bigoted, credulous, or just plain obnoxious or offensive. We are at a crossroads, and must ask ourselves, what is the Church? What is it for?

What is the Church? The Church has been understood over the years in several ways. One of the more recent is the Church as a business. Sometimes even people in the Church talk about it as if it were a store. We refer to "shopping for a church." Our vestries employ best "business practices"; clergy and staff are "hired" and "paid salaries," and so forth. And yet the New Testament never talks about the Church in those terms. Rather, it describes the Church as a community of people, a family or household, a tribe, a nation, and so forth, not anything remotely like a business, but a *community*.

Another way we have been understood over the years is as a hierarchy—and only the hierarchy. Thus "joining the Church" used to mean, not baptism, but taking monastic vows or being ordained. But again the New Testament knows nothing of the sort. The Church of the New Testament is a community of *equals*. With different skills and ministries, yes, but equals.

Another image of the Church over the years is as a political institution, *de facto* ruling and governing the people—all the people, for baptism was then practically compulsory. We were understood to be something like government in God's name, or the divine aspect of the government—either way, there is no such thing envisioned in the New Testament; there the Church is, instead, a group of people *at odds* with the powers and principalities that rule the world and destroy God's creatures. Not a government, but the "green shoots" of a different sort of world: The Reign of God, confronting the establishment and its cultural values.

We have also pictured the Church over the years, especially since the Enlightenment, as a collection of individuals having individual "private" spiritual experiences, disconnected from society; a Church in which the teachings of Christ are "spiritualized" and held with no effect on our wider political and social life. Again, the New Testament knows nothing of that sort. Instead, it paints a picture of a community of people with a view of the world on the brink of its final healing or, if you prefer, "salvation," and an ethos or way of living in such a "New World."[1]

---

1 The phrase "New World," which in the Syriac tradition refers to the Reign of God, was used by the first Spanish invaders to designate the Americas, for they hoped to be agents of the establishment of God's Reign in the new lands. The disastrous results are a warning to anyone who thinks that the Reign of God can coexist with violence and genocide.

Finally, in the extremes of individualism, to "be Christian" has come to mean agreeing with some supposedly Christian *ideas* as if the Church were nothing more than a library. So, we have a large percentage of the population in the United States claiming to be "Christian" while never darkening the door of a church. Not so in the New Testament, where to be Christian was to be part of a community, regularly participating actively in its rites and service to the world, often at great personal cost.

As a result of all these misconceptions, people expect a hierarchical business that will sell you a smorgasbord of private, individual "spiritual" goods and experiences to be had individually, while telling you what to think and do. No wonder newcomers often tell me with amazed eyes, "I have been coming to Bible study for a couple of months and I can't get over the fact that no one has told me what to think." Good. We are most of all interested in what *you* make of a biblical passage and how it may apply to your life.

What is the Church supposed to be? Gathering together the New Testament's understandings of the Church mentioned above, we can form the following image: We are to be a community of people, gathering regularly, locally; a family, a household, a tribe, a nation and yes, a body—the Body of Christ, his continuation in history. Our liturgies define us that way; especially baptism, which *constitutes* us that way as limbs (members) of Christ's risen Body. St. Paul literally got knocked off his horse by the insight that the Christian community is Christ himself. "Saul, Saul, why do you persecute me?" he heard a voice telling him as he galloped back to Damascus after persecuting Christians (Acts 9:4). And like Jesus our Head, we are a human Body, with all its characteristic human ways of being a social body, but a Body in whom God's love and healing project for the world are proclaimed, gratefully received, and worked toward.

The Church as a sign. Although liturgy is made up of signs or significant actions carrying a multiplicity of meanings, the Church itself is also a sign, symbol, or icon. The New Testament often uses the phrase "first fruits" as a metaphor for something new and wonderful taking place, such as the resurrection of Jesus, "the first fruits of those who are asleep" (1 Corinthians 15:20).[2] Today we might say "green shoots." The Church also, as Body of the risen Christ, shares in this, receiving the Spirit as evidence of the nearness of God's Reign.

Anthropologists of ritual tell us that it presents an experience of how life *ought to be* and reconciles our failure to live that way with the ideal. Applied to worship, liturgy presents, or ought to present, an

---

2 In turn, Paul is using the Old Testament commandment to offer the first fruits of the harvest to God.

experience of life as it ought to be, lived with and before God. This is the eschatological dimension of Christian worship, in which the Reign is already present, though it has not arrived yet.

What is it for? The Church exists for the sake of the world, and not to take us out of it. If it does, for an hour every Sunday, it is only to send us right back again on mission: to proclaim, by deeds and words if necessary, the Good News of the nearness of the Reign. For the gospel is not merely the story about Jesus; it is hard to imagine him saying to the crowds, "I was born of a virgin, in a stable and these three foreigners came with weird presents," or "I taught the teachers at the temple." No. The gospel of Jesus Christ is what he went around saying: "The Reign of God is very near; change your hearts and trust the Good News."

Perhaps no other story in the New Testament encapsulates the answer to the question, "What is the Church for?" than the event on Pentecost. Wind and fire, Luke writes, came into the upper room where the disciples were gathered on the fiftieth day (pentecost) after Passover (Acts 2). Wind and fire also accompanied God's manifestation on Sinai and the giving of the Law, still remembered and celebrated by Jews to this day on the same fiftieth day, Shavuot. It was the wind and fire of God's own breath of life, or Spirit, empowering the disciples with the new Law. Each and every one. Incidentally, the account does not say that Peter's (or Mary's) tongue of fire was larger, or that one was better at languages than another. Rather, the story stresses the Spirit coming upon a community of people. They ran out talking about what they had experienced *as a group.*

The Spirit also immediately made them translators in all languages, so that each person hearing them did so *"in their own tongue."* The story moves from a special event in the upper room among a few disciples toward something world-wide, multilingual, multicultural, multi-national. The agenda of the story is fairly obvious: the Good News of the Reign of God, inaugurated by Jesus in his life, death, and rising again and the giving of God's own Breath was not just for Judaeans but for *all nations,* and so naturally the disciples had to announce it in all languages. The Breath (Spirit) of God moved them to go beyond their own cultural and linguistic boundaries, and they became bridges between the religion of Israel and its Christian transformation into something global. In the process, this once fearful, secluded community further articulated its reason for being and its mission.

The incarnation of the Church in cultures. We are accustomed by now to talk of the "other": that person who is not like you, and whose difference is very often taken as an excuse for exclusion, belittling, harassment, even murder. The list grows by the year: women, African Americans, Latinos, Native Americans,

Asian Americans, Haitian Americans, the differently-abled, refugees of color, LGBTQ persons, and so on. We rightly want to include all sorts of people in the Church, as Jesus would, not only a wide variety of Americans but people from many different cultures. This brings up the relationship of worship to the culture(s) in which it takes place.

Like the disciples, we too must translate the Good News of the Reign and its manifestation in worship in ways people can actually understand, into their own language, culture, mores, and proclivities. This was one of the driving forces of the Protestant Reformation, as the worship of the Church had become alien and incomprehensible to the average person. We are not quite in such a dismal situation liturgically yet, but we are headed that way.

In keeping with the Anglican tradition of having different styles of worship appropriate to different contexts, we cannot insist on imposing, say, Anglo worship in a Latino congregation in Guatemala. If we insist, Anglicanism will not be catholic in the sense of being universal, but one cultural form imposing itself throughout the world. Anglican liturgy has been there and done that, with disastrous results. We *must* translate because one cannot have a conversation that begins with "I have something great to tell you but first you must be more like me and speak my language."

This means that we as a community, the Church, will have to take flesh—become incarnate—in a given people, language, nation, or culture to be able to proclaim the Good News of the Reign. Incarnation, however, is much like learning a second language. It is hard and takes a long time before one is truly fluent. For one thing, learning *a second language, let alone another culture, always involves being partially in the dark,* groping for words and being grateful for constant correction by true new friends, acclimating to the vertigo of opening your mouth with no assurance that what you are saying is in any way correct.

Reaching out to communicate with the "other" is therefore always fraught with danger, fear, humility, not-knowing, blind guessing, and so forth, and difficult for people who must always be right. This is true about reaching out to those whose appearance and experiences are different from our own as well as to white, straight, Anglo non-Christians, *suspicious of religion.* We must learn to communicate, not because we must grow numerically in order to be financially viable, but because our community, like our worship, is a *sign* and signs are supposed to communicate. As with language, we cannot ask those outside our community to be first more like us and learn the meaning of our liturgy; we will have to learn their "language" of worship: their secular language of gathering, listening, sharing meaning, praying, giving thanks, eating together, and commissioning. At the very least, we will have to make sure that our ritual actions are crystal clear to them. This brings up the question of Christian *evangelism.*

Evangelization vs. evangelism. Evangelism is often described in Church circles as "sharing our faith in Jesus." The gospel (evangel, from *euangelion* or Good News) was the announcement of an impending *radical change for the better,* but has by now often become the sharing of our subjective love and commitment to Jesus. And that is fine, as long as it is accompanied by the Good News of the nearness of the Reign.

Who wants to hear this Good News? Well, the people who live their lives in daily bad news: the poor, homeless, destitute; the abused, ignored, discriminated against; the sick, old, and despairing; the nobodies, the invisible, those of no account; the foreigners, refugees, LGBTQ persons, women. You get the picture. They are *starving* for good news.

Frankly, however, "sharing your faith in Jesus," without bringing tangible good news to them, will accomplish very little, for prattle about Jesus is not good news to them. For them good news may include jobs, a roof over their heads, income; safety, acknowledgement, acceptance; medical care, respect, and hope; protection from deportation and children in cages; full equality for LGBTQ persons, recognition of women's authority. This is the true agenda of the Church: proclaiming the Good News of the closeness of the Reign of God *tangibly,* for all to see and feel, and not simply increasing our membership by finding customers of our spiritual goods. We are a community, not a store.

In order to give the Good News its power, we will have to engage in this *at the local level,* not only within our Church community (good place to start!) but in the surrounding world as well.

The meaning of the Church community. We can explore the meaning of the Church (*to whom?*) generally, but in fact, the Church is not an abstraction, but a concrete group of people in a particular place and time. So we may want to ask ourselves, what is the meaning of our Church (parish) community? For you? For other congregants? For your bishop and diocese? For your neighborhood and town? We constantly assume it: "That's not us," someone will say, implying that there is a notion, somewhere, of who we are and what we are all about.

Perhaps the most basic and universal experience of community we have as humans is our belonging to a family of origin. What does our family of origin mean? *To whom?* My family of origin means something to me, inseparable from my relationships with them over geography and time, but perhaps something quite different to a sibling, or a niece. Now take a look at your church. Three services. Membership about two hundred. What do you all mean to yourselves, to each other, to the neighbors, to your town? To the secular atheists who assume all

Christians are right-wing fundamentalists? To the six-year-old brought here by her undocumented Mexican mother? The local Christian community is a living *icon* to itself and to the surrounding world. First in importance is the meaning of our community *to ourselves*. Without that there can be no social cohesion and we run the risk of gathering on Sundays, but like a dysfunctional family, developing all manner of problematic behaviors rising from not knowing who we are, or what we are about, or to what end.

Then there is our meaning to our fellow citizens. Here we are in deep, deep *trouble*. For in our culture "Christian" has increasingly come to mean "intolerant," "bigoted," "deluded," "patriarchal," and much worse. At the very least this means that their perception of us does not match our perception of ourselves; actually, it is its *opposite*. How did we come to this? How did the icon that is the Christian community come to be identified with *oppression*? The process is the topic of another book, but the question remains: If our worship expresses what and who we are as a community of the Reign of God, how might it do so better, in more transparent and culturally appropriate ways? What do we have to develop, adapt, and change to make our meeting and eating with God, our incorporation into Christ in baptism, and our other rites more transparent, presenting a vision of life with God *here* in the coming Reign?

There is no general prescription, as one size will not fit all, if for no other reason that our Church is increasingly varied, multicultural, and multilingual. Still, two general observations are apropos: First, the liturgy is clearly not the doings of clergy only, but of the whole assembly, led by a variety of ministers. And although rectors have the power and responsibility to design worship at the local level, it is foolhardy to do so without some structured way of receiving input from congregants. We need to listen more closely to the answers given by the most recent newcomers, when we asked, "How do *you* gather, listen, share meaning? How do *you* pray, give thanks, eat together, and get commissioned? The answer, dear reader, cannot be given across the board, the same for every congregation. Instead, it lies with you, in your hands and your priest's, called to fashion liturgy locally in more transparent ways, in conversation with twenty centuries of tradition. For the worship of the Christian community is not a commodity created in a central factory and reproduced identically at the local congregation like a frozen dinner out of the microwave, but the way we meet and eat with God, in our very human ways.

And this brings us back to the original meaning of the term "liturgy." For *leitourgia*, in Greek, meant public works done *in service to the community*. Our liturgy as a succession of sign-actions when we assemble for eucharist and other rites is not complete by itself. It needs its second aspect: service to the world.

It has been an honor having you visit the *House of Meanings* for this conversation. Now, go out into the world to heal it!

A Postscript
on Liturgical Design

We can no longer assume that liturgical planning comes ready-made, either from the bishop's cathedral or the seminary. Rather, learning from these, local congregations will have to engage in designing their worship—using the Church's textual tools of course, but in ways appropriate to their own situations and local cultures. How does one do this? Allow me to give an example of a process, rather than a one-size-for-all prescription.

It is spring of 1990 at St. Mark's in Palo Alto, California, in Silicon Valley. The congregation includes early techies, young and old, lawyers, a city councilman. It is mostly white except for two or three people of color, and this gay Latino. Easter is approaching. The worship committee gathers to plan the liturgies of Holy Week. This is how we planned the Easter Vigil:

First we decided to have it before dawn, ending with a festive breakfast with dancing. Then the question came up: Where should we light the fire? Palo Alto enjoys wonderful weather in April. "Outside, of course!" We would light the fire and the candle outside and then go in. "Why go in? It's going to be lovely; who wants to go *in*?" someone said, and so we decided that after the Easter Proclamation, we would read the lessons around the fire. "Do we have to read them? It will be dark, and boring." We did read Genesis, but the Sacrifice of Isaac was told as a story from Sara's vantage point. Interestingly, the rendition included every word of the biblical text, which the storyteller had memorized.

Next, the baptisms. We had a family—two adults and their two girls. "Will we baptize them outside too?"—No. too chilly for that. So inside. How? "Not in a birdbath! Full immersion, please." What? How? Where? "I'll build a baptismal font large enough," a brave assistant rector offered. And so he did—of plywood, sealed and painted with marine varnish inside and out, a sort of sarcophagus, with steps leading up to it and down into the water. Where to put it? "Why not in the middle of the nave—among the people that the candidates are joining!" But the pews. . . "Take out the pews!" Eight electric screwdrivers later, the pews would be gone and stored.

They would return later, after the Vigil, for we were not ready for a permanent change. Gone. "Wait: where are people going to sit, on the floor?" We asked everyone to bring carpets. Chairs were provided around the perimeter of the space for those who needed them.

"How do we get from the fire to the font?" A procession! What do we sing? "Psalm 42, As the deer yearns for living water," of course. And so we did. The baptismal candidates came in at the end of the procession, into a building almost empty with only the font in the midst of a carpeted floor—looking a bit like a mosque. Around the font stood the congregation, welcoming them.

The candidates turned to the darkness outside as they were asked, "Do you reject Satan . . ." and so forth. And as they were asked, "Do you turn to Christ?" they turned toward the font and the congregation.

We proceeded with the baptisms and the anointings. While they were dressing, we had a conversation about the decorations on the font, painted by the Sunday school children: the Baptism of Jesus, the Samaritan Woman, the Healing of the Paralytic, the Anointing of David—mostly stories heard during the previous Sundays (Lent in liturgical Year A).

The baptized family came back, beaming, and we welcomed them into the household of God with applause, hugs, and kisses. As they approached the

one presiding proclaimed, "Alleluia, Christ is Risen!"
honoring them with incense and bowing to them.

The epistle was read, then a psalm sung, and the
Easter gospel proclaimed. The eucharist, at a round
altar around which we could all stand together. We
filed out after being sent out, by the deacon, led by a
band into a festive breakfast of roast lamb, and much
more.

I do not write this so you can try to reproduce
it, but to illustrate a *process*. Notice that throughout
a group of people were *talking to each other* about
how to celebrate the Vigil. Who were this group,
you may well ask? It was what we called the *liturgy
team:* the rector and deacon(s), music director/or-
ganist, the head of the altar guild, the coordinator of
readers, the coordinator of acolytes, the head usher.
Often there were also two or three members of the
congregation as well. We met about every month or
six weeks to plan a liturgical *season*—not so much
individual liturgies—Holy Week excepted. We did
not micromanage, arguing about which frontal to
use. The altar guild decided that. We kept our eyes
on the big picture, with questions like, "What images does the lectionary for the coming season offer
us? How do we integrate them into the rest of the
liturgical experience? What do we want say, Lent, to
feel like? Besides a change in the color of vestments,
should we also change the incense? The taste of locally baked bread? The wine? What seating arrange-

ment do we envision? How will we decorate the space? Might the liturgies be celebrated outdoors? Do we need additional volunteers to carry this out?" and so on.

This sort of conversation also gave the music director and the altar guild a feeling and a set of ideas and attitudes to aid them in making their decisions, and bringing them to the rector for final approval.

We found that several virtues helped: We quickly learned that without trusting each other we could not work together and keep our eyes on the whole liturgical experience for a season, succumbing instead to micromanagement. We learned to delegate to each other. The readers did not tell the musician what hymns to choose, but trusted him to do it. The deacon did not solve every acolyte's quandary, but trusted their coordinator to handle that. It was true teamwork, under the wise leadership of a rector who trusted us.

Should you try this? Probably; I do not know. What I do know is that whenever I have engaged in this sort of liturgical planning the laity have become much more excited and enthusiastic about being the Church at prayer.

Glossary

Throughout *A House of Meanings*, you may have been surprised by my choice of meanings of familiar words, such as gospel, church, and so forth. Perhaps it is because over the centuries the original, wider range of meanings of the terms we employ as Christians has solidified into ever narrower interpretations, losing the original "flavor" of the term. This glossary seeks to reverse the process, providing, for our most common terminology, the original—mostly Greek—range of meaning. I am indebted to David Bentley Hart for his excellent, in-depth glossary at the end of his translation of the New Testament.[1]

---

1 David Bentley Hart, *The New Testament* (New Haven: Yale University Press, 2017).

baptism. Gr: *baptisma*. Lit., "immersion."

belief. Gr: *pistis*. Lit., "trusting allegiance" trusting faith," as in, "I have faith in you, son."

bishop. Gr: *episkopos*. Lit., "overseer," "supervisor."

Church. Gr: *ekklesia*. Lit., "an assembly called out, or elected." In ancient Greece, an elected body of legislators.

deacon. Gr: *diakonos*. Lit., "one who walks through dust," a servant.

gospel. Gr: *euangelion*. Lit., "good message," "good announcement, or "Good News." The Good News of the impending arrival of the Reign of God.

elect. Gr: *proorizen*. To mark out in advance; to preordain.

eternal life. Gr: *zoe aionios*. Lit., the life of the Age of the Reign of God here on earth, inaugurated by Jesus's resurrection; an age lasting a very long time, possibly forever.

eucharist. Gr: *eucharistia*. Lit., "thanksgiving."

hell/Hell. Gr: *hades*. "The underworld." in Heb.: *sheol*. Gr: *Tartaros* (used once). A subterranean prison where the fallen angels and demons are held until judgment day. Gr: *Gehenna*. The Valley of the Hinnon outside Jerusalem. A place associated by Jews with ancient pagan child sacrifice. A charnel ground. Jerusalem's rubbish dump, always on fire. In rabbinical schools, metaphor for a place of *temporary* purification after death.

Kingdom (Reign) of God. Gr: *basileia theou*.
The kingship, or royal authority, of God.
This world under God's rule, characterized
by *shalom*, a healed world of truth, justice,
peace, and love. In Matthew, "the Kingdom of
Heaven" on earth.

liturgy. Gr: *leitourgia*. Lit., "work for the people."
"Public works," as in roads, bridges, and so
forth, "public service," later "the public service at the temple."

ordination. Gr: *Chairotonia*, Lit., "laying on of
hands."

priest. (1). Old French: *Presbytere*, contraction
preste, from Gr: *presbyteros*. Lit., "old man,
old person, elder." A member of a town
council *(sanhedrin)* in Judea. In the earliest churches, closer to our members of the
vestry. (2). Gr: *hiereus*. Temple leader who
offered sacrifices (qv). In the New Testament
the term is applied only to Christ.

ransom. Gr: *lutron* or *antilutron*. The required
payment for the emancipation of a slave, paid
by Christ not to God but to death. The price
of liberation.

repentance. Gr: *metanoia*. Lit., "a change or
transformation of the heart/mind" (the ancients did not separate the two).

sacrifice. Gr: *thusia*. A sacred offering to God,
not necessarily by slaughtering an animal.

salvation. Gr: *soteria*. Lat.: *salus*. Rescue. First
used of Moses freeing the slaves; safeguard-
ing, liberation, healing.

Second Coming, the. In the original Greek:
parousia. The visit of a dignitary to inspect a
city.

sin. Anglo Saxon: *synn.* "Law-breaking," "crime,"
translated from the Gr., *hamartia,* Lit., "missing the target," (as in archery) "erring," "making a mistake." Lat.: *peccatum,* "A stumble,"
"a tripping," "a false step."

Spirit. Gr: *pneuma.* Breath or wind.